PLANTS OF COLONIAL WILLIAMSBURG

Plants of Colonial Williamsburg

HOW TO IDENTIFY 200
OF COLONIAL AMERICA'S FLOWERS,
HERBS, AND TREES

By Joan Parry Dutton

With illustrations by Marion Ruff Sheehan

Published by
The Colonial Williamsburg Foundation
WILLIAMSBURG, VIRGINIA

© 1979 by

THE COLONIAL WILLIAMSBURG FOUNDATION
Third Printing, 1986

Library of Congress Cataloging in Publication Data

Dutton, Joan Parry.

    Plants of Colonial Williamsburg

    Bibliography: p. 179
    Includes index.

      1. Botany—Virginia—Williamsburg. 2. Plants,
Ornamental—Virginia—Williamsburg—Identification.
3. Plant introduction—Virginia—Williamsburg. 4. Williamsburg, Va.—Description—Guidebooks.   I. Colonial
Williamsburg Foundation.   II. Title.

QK191.D87   581.9'755'4252   76-50633
ISBN 0-87935-042-3
The zone map that appears on the endpapers is repro-
duced from Norman Taylor, ed., *Taylor's Encyclopedia of
Gardening,* 4th ed., © renewed 1976 by Margaretta
Taylor, with the kind permission of the Houghton Mifflin
Company.

Printed in the United States of America

Contents

Acknowledgments

Although my name is attached to this handbook, I regard the making of it as a team effort. I wish to record my thanks to those members of the staff of the Colonial Williamsburg Foundation who have given so much, in their own kindly ways, of their time and patience. I am especially indebted to Donna M. E. Ware and to the late Alice M. Coats. Dr. Ware, curator of the herbarium at the College of William and Mary, reviewed the botanical nomenclature. Miss Coats, one of England's foremost authorities on the history of plants and of plant explorers, gave me permission to repeat some of the intriguing and amusing associations of people with plants that her own many years of research have revealed and her several books have already recorded. Finally, I am also especially indebted to the late Dr. Raymond Taylor. His *Plants of Colonial Days* introduced thousands of visitors to the plants in Colonial Williamsburg.

Introduction

Plants in profusion and variety, both native and imported, grow in and around the Historic Area of Williamsburg in Virginia. Large and small, rare and common, trees and shrubs, flowers and vines, vegetables, fruits, and herbs—one could count more than 500 different species.

In this book you will find about 200 of them briefly described and illustrated. All the varieties included can be seen growing, one year or another, in the gardens of Colonial Williamsburg, and all were known to colonial gardeners or to their British contemporaries.

Trespassers against this last rule—plants growing in the Historic Area that shouldn't be there, it would seem—may be explained and justified on the following grounds:

First, the "colonial" period—for the purpose of this book—extends to 1820. Although the Revolution slowed the exchange of plants between Europe and North America, the pause was temporary. By 1820, however, plant collectors had largely shifted their searching to the Middle West and the Pacific Coast, and the first great era of plant exploration in the New World had come to an end.

Second, some plants introduced into England from elsewhere in the mid to late eighteenth century probably did not reach North America, or were not commonly grown here, until sometime after the Revolution. Hence, some of the plants described in this book may not have appeared in Williamsburg before 1776 or may have been introduced by the twentieth-century researchers of eighteenth-century plant materials who were responsible for the replanting of the Historic Area in the 1930s.

Finally, while species brought in from the wild presented no problem of authenticity, since they had persisted unchanged by cultivation, it was another matter with plants of garden origin. Most of the cultivars (the named horticultural varieties) known in the eighteenth century have since disappeared, their places taken by modern varieties and hybrids—some of which perforce appear in the recreated gardens.

This, however, is not a botanical manual. Aside from a few words of description, the chief clues to plant identification will be found in the illustrations. The emphasis of the text falls on plant history and origin. As Maurice Maeterlinck once wrote, plants have "a long human past behind them. They are the immortals, the living things that tie together our forefathers' yesterdays and our todays, as they link our own time with endless tomorrows."

Plant Exchange between the Old World and the New

The recorded history of British plant exploration in North America properly begins with the first and second Roanoke voyages that preceded the founding of Jamestown. In 1584 Sir Walter Raleigh dispatched two small ships under the command of captains Philip Amadas and Arthur Barlow to explore the land lying behind the Carolina Outer Banks, the chain of islands stretching from the Virginia Capes to below Cape Lookout.

The following year, Raleigh sent out England's first colonizing expedition. Accompanying it were Thomas Hariot, mathematician and naturalist, and John White, artist and cartographer. Together they were to record the plants, birds, fish, and Indian life of the new Virginia. Roanoke Island, in the sound between the Outer Banks and mainland North Carolina, was chosen as the place for settlement. There the colonists stayed some ten months, from August 1585 to June 1586.

That June, Francis Drake, after sacking Spanish settlements in the Caribbean, made contact with the Roanoke colony. A storm that raged for nearly four days just as fresh stores were to be landed came as a last straw: the colonists gladly accepted Drake's offer to take them home. In the tempestuous embarkation, Hariot managed to hold onto his notes and White saved some of his drawings of Indian life and of plants, animals, insects, and birds. Seventy-five of these watercolor drawings survive in the British Museum.

Although New World plants had reached Europe before 1600, some through Drake, some through Spain and from New France (Canada), it was the founding of Jamestown and Plymouth that opened doorways to a vast unexplored wilderness and the eagerly sought floral wealth within it. Traffic in plants between the Old World and the New began, but all through the seventeenth century—during the first one hundred years of settlement—many English and Europeans found the introduction of New World plants frustratingly slow and sporadic. Comparatively few reached them before John Bartram began collecting in the eighteenth century, then traffic in plants gradually increased up to and beyond the Revolution.

To Virginia, from the Old World, came plants that Europe had grown for centuries, as well as those but newly brought in from the Orient by way of the ships of the English and Dutch trading companies or along the caravan route from China to St. Petersburg and thence to France. Back to England from Virginia went plants of a new flora that rivaled China's, plants that, in their turn, were sent out all over the world.

Broadly speaking, most of the fruit trees, vegetables, and herbs belong to the Old World, as do most of the flowering bulbs. In addition to tobacco, corn, and a few other vegetables, North America's great contribution are its trees and flowering shrubs and vines; many of its wild flowers have long since become standby perennials of the English flower garden.

Williamsburg has a very special place in North America's garden history. It was the home, or the rendezvous, of several notable plant collectors and ardent gardeners. Some prominent Englishmen who shared these common interests also had direct ties with the Virginia colony although they themselves never crossed the Atlantic.

This is not to suggest that any large number of interested persons took part in the exchange and study of plants. In fact, the number of people concerned was, on the whole, remarkably small, which is why the members of the European–North American fraternity knew each other so well. For most of them, the science of botany and the cultivation of foreign plants—exotics as they were called—were but two facets of their absorbing interest in the "curiosities" of nature. Many a plant collector was a well-rounded naturalist. Along with seeds and plants from the New World went stuffed birds, shells, animal skins, wasp nests, snakes and fish preserved in wine, and many other items that caught an observer's eye. Few of these naturalists met face-to-face. Most knew one another, and some became close friends, solely through correspondence. Peter Collinson of London was, perhaps, the kingpin, the confluence of contacts among them. He was an indefatigable correspondent. In a letter that he wrote to John Custis of Williamsburg in December 1735, he referred to his fellow gardeners as "Wee Brothers of the Spade."

Brief biographical sketches of some of the plant collectors, garden enthusiasts, and early garden writers whose names appear in this book will be found in the Appendix. Three influential and often mentioned groups—the Royal Society of London, the Company of Gardeners, and the Society of Gardeners—are also discussed there.

How Plants Got Their Names

Botany, the science of plant life, has its own glossary. Begun when Latin was still the international language most widely used by scientists and learned men in Europe, this glossary is in Latin—not classical Latin but an expanded form used since the Middle Ages for many purposes. Plant names stem from other languages, many from the Greek. Along with geographical and personal names, these plant names were, and still are, "latinized" in botanical writing.

Up to the time that Linnaeus established his binomial system, botanists recognized plants by names that amounted to long Latin descriptions. For example, John Parkinson called rhubarb *Hippolapathum maximum rotundifolium exoticum.*

The Linnaean system simplified plant nomenclature. Each wild plant was given two Latin names, and two only: a generic name (or surname) that is placed first with a capital initial letter, and a specific (or identifying Christian) name. Linnaeus replaced Parkinson's title for rhubarb by *Rheum rhaponticum. Rheum* evolved from an old name for medicinal rhubarb, while *rhaponticum* referred to that kind of rhubarb found growing in the Black Sea area.

A number of closely related genera compose a family; a genus may be defined as a collection of closely related species; and a species is a group of individual plants that have the same common and distinctive structural characteristics, although they may vary in color of flower and size of leaf. The genus name may be common to a number of plants, as in the several species of *Rosa, Lilium,* and *Delphinium,* but the specific name defines the individual kind of plant, as with *Rosa palustris, Lilium canadense,* or *Delphinium consolida.* These plants are species, alike wherever found and reliably true to type from seed.

Specific names often provide clues to the country of

origin or to a plant's characteristics. *Sinensis* and *chinensis* mean "of China"; *alba, rosea,* and *caerulea* mean white, pink, and blue respectively.

The names of some genera are adaptations of the old Greek and Latin names of plants. Some describe the plant—for example, *Helianthus* combines two Greek words meaning "sun" and "flower," an appropriate name for the genus that includes sunflowers. Linnaeus was very apt at choosing appropriate names.

The name of the person who first named and described a given plant species follows the scientific name of the plant, sometimes in abbreviated form. For instance, in the citation *"Cornus florida* L." *Cornus* is the genus name, *florida* is the species name, and "L." is the abbreviation of the last name of the famous Swedish botanist Carolus Linnaeus, who named this species. In other cases two names may be given after the scientific name of a particular plant, the first name being enclosed in parentheses, and the second not. An example is the pinxter flower azalea. Linnaeus was the person who first named this plant entity, but he called it *Azalea nudiflora* L. Later, John Torrey decided that this species rightfully belonged in the genus Rhododendron and its name became *Rhododendron nudiflorum* (L.) Torr. This method of citation gives credit both to the botanist who first named the plant and to the botanist who may later decide that a new interpretation of relationships dictates its placement in another genus.

Over the years the development of science has resulted in much reclassification of certain plants and resultant changes in plant names. This has led to an extensive synonymy of names. Some synonyms are given in the text: for example, cherry-laurel, *Prunus caroliniana* (syn. *Laurocerasus caroliniana*). Yet, for all the reclassification, the underlying principles of the Linnaean system remain.

As for common names, these are often confusing. Any one plant may be known by many different common names, and some common names are applied to wholly different plants—both in their native land and in other countries. When we remember this, the advantage of plants having one universal scientific name that is recognized by gardeners the world over is obvious.

To avoid repetition, the meaning of certain specific names that occur over and over again in the following pages are given here:

canada, canadensis	general region north of Virginia
decidua*	deciduous, losing leaves in wintertime
florida	full of flowers
occidentalis	western
officinalis	official, of the shop, of the apothecary; of use, of service to man
orientalis	from the Orient
perennis	perennial
sempervirens	evergreen
virginiana, virginica	Virginia, a region in eastern North America extending far beyond the present boundaries of the state

Family Names

All plant families have scientific names that have been formed by appending the suffix -aceae to the stem of the name of a particular genus of each family. The name Primulaceae (Primrose family), for example, is based on the generic name *Primula*. There are eight families, however, which have long possessed a name formed differently from the standard method described above. These older names, also considered valid according to the *International Code of Botanical Nomenclature* (1972) on the basis of

---

* All plants in this handbook are deciduous except those described as evergreen.

long usage and wide acceptance, are listed below, along with the newer conforming -*aceae* counterparts. The name of the genus on which each of the latter is based is given in parentheses.

Palm family: Arecaceae (*Areca*) = Palmae
Grass family: Poaceae (*Poa*) = Gramineae
Mustard family: Brassicaceae (*Brassica*) = Cruciferae
Pea family: Fabaceae (*Faba*) = Leguminosae
St. Johnswort family: Hypericaceae (*Hypericum*) = Guttiferae
Celery family: Apiaceae (*Apium*) = Umbelliferae
Mint family: Lamiaceae (*Lamium*) = Labiatae
Aster family: Asteraceae (*Aster*) = Compositae

Many recent botanical publications use the traditional names, while others may list both names in the family headings, but in this country the exclusive use of the -*aceae* names is gaining in acceptance.[1] For the sake of clarity, both names for each of these eight families are given in this book.

Plant Introduction Dates

Almost all of the plant introduction dates given in this book apply to England. Far more is known about the first significant appearance of foreign plants in England than about their arrival in the American colonies. In many instances, nevertheless, the date given is subject to conjecture, and it may even conflict with the date of reintroduction of a plant that had died out.

Several garden dictionaries give 1596 and 1629 as the dates for the introduction into England of a number of plants, suggesting that an unusual number of shipments

---

[1] For example, Albert E. Radford, Harry E. Ahles, and C. Ritchie Bell, *Manual of the Vascular Flora of the Carolinas* (Chapel Hill, N. C., 1968), and Robert W. Long and Olga Lakela, *A Flora of Tropical Florida: A Manual of the Seed Plants and Ferns of Southern Peninsular Florida* (Coral Gables, Fla., 1971).

arrived during those two years. In fact, the two dates are those when two books containing the earliest references to the plants in question—John Gerard's *Catalogus arborum, fructicum ac planatarum* (1596) and John Parkinson's *Paradisi in Sole, Paradisus Terrestris* (1629)—were published. More correctly the dates should be given as "before 1596" and "before 1629."

"Florists' Flowers"

The word "florist" is generally accepted to mean one who sells cut flowers and ornamental plants for indoor decoration. In England in earlier times a florist was also a gardener, and the plants a gardener-florist selected and hybridized were known as "florists' flowers." Even in the seventeenth century, skillful gardeners in England, France, and the Netherlands cultivated certain flowers—pinks, tulips, and auriculas—to a rare perfection that only a select clientele could afford.

By the late eighteenth century the newly introduced plants, particularly those from North America, were in vogue, and the old familiars were out of favor—except among the industrial population. John Claudius Loudon, writing in his classic *Encyclopaedia of Gardening* in 1824, said that the edged auricula was "like the Tulip, Pink, etc., a poor man's flower, and a fine blow is rarely to be seen in the gardens of the nobility and the gentry."

In the tiny, sooty backyards in and around Britain's manufacturing districts, weavers and other working-class artisans brought the old florists' flowers to new standards of perfection in the early nineteenth century. Sometimes, as Loudon pointed out, they were "boxed in with all kinds of glass cases, even in areas on a level with a coal-hole." Floral societies were formed, and stringent rules were drawn up for showing at prize exhibitions. Rivalry to excel no doubt played its part, but gardening and devotion to one or another flower was the working man's chief recreation.

[9]

Eight flowers were named florists' flowers by the florists' societies: the tulip, auricula, carnation, pink, anemone, ranunculus, hyacinth, and polyanthus. Once the choice flowers of the Jacobean court, these were now cottage garden favorites, and the backyard garden of industrial areas was their stronghold. The silk weavers at Spitalfields, near London, specialized in auriculas and tulips, and those of Manchester in auriculas and polyanthus, while Norwich was noted for carnations and Paisley for pinks. The laced pinks of Paisley are close contemporaries of the Paisley shawl: the same hands that tended the flowers made the shawls and, observed Loudon, the weavers' "attention to raising flowers contributed to improve their invention in elegant fancy muslins."

Fruits and Vegetables

This handbook includes only some of the plants to be seen in the Historic Area. Vegetables are excluded, as are the commonly grown fruit trees—these are familiar to most people the country over.

Yet a book on plants known in colonial days surely should make some mention of vegetables and fruits, for they stood at the top of the colonial gardener's want list. Besides, most Williamsburg gardens in colonial days were vegetable gardens with a small orchard adjoining them. Gardeners such as Thomas Jefferson, George Washington, and John Custis of Williamsburg cultivated not only vegetables and fruits but also plants considered desirable because they were curious and rare or possessed ornamental qualities. In that respect they differed from the majority of Virginia planters and from most Williamsburg home gardeners.

The demand for vegetable seeds, referred to as "garden seeds," far outstripped that for other plants, as the long and detailed advertisements of "garden seeds . . . just imported" in the *Virginia Gazette* plainly show. Christopher Ayscough, gardener to Governor Francis Fauquier, and Thomas Crease, gardener to the College of William and Mary, advertised their fresh supplies—as did others. One of Ayscough's advertisements listed, along with cauliflowers, broccoli, onions, leeks, celery, and so forth, seven kinds of cabbage, six of peas, five of beans, and five of lettuce.

Two prominent Williamsburg citizens, Judge Joseph Prentis and John Randolph, king's attorney, left records of their interest in growing vegetables (see biographical notes). Thomas Jefferson took as much satisfaction in jotting down in his Garden Book when peas were in blossom and pod as in noting "Carnations in full life." All three men grew what we today consider to be out of the ordinary vegetables that included asparagus, Jerusalem artichokes, okra, eggplant, and salsify.

Fruits were also of prime importance, not only for the making of pies and other sweetmeats, but for making cordials, cider, and beer. In his *Account of Virginia . . .* (1676), Thomas Glover wrote: "As to fruit trees . . . few planters but that have fair and large orchards, some whereof have 1200 trees and upward bearing all sorts of English apples . . . of which they made great store of cider . . . likewise great peach-orchards, which bear such an infinite quantity of peaches, that at some plantations they beat down to the Hoggs fourty bushels in a year." Virginia ham and peach brandy were two Virginia specialties that the colonists sent "home" to England. St. George Tucker sent his recipe for brandied peaches to his daughter, Mrs. Frances Coalter.

Cherries ranked next in popularity after apples and peaches. Plums were cultivated on a limited scale as were many other fruits. The choicest plum of all time, the greengage, was also grown. Mark Catesby's sister Elizabeth, who had married Dr. William Cocke of Williamsburg, secretary of the colony, wrote to one of her family that while she was visiting friends, "I met with the Green

Gage plumb so much celebrated of late years. I've sent you some of the stones." Quantities of fruit trees were raised by planting the seeds or "stone" and by grafting.

A word on herbs: the ones included in this book are those Judge Prentis and others grew in Williamsburg and the immediate neighborhood.

Plant Hardiness

Finally, for those readers who want to know if they can grow certain plants in their home localities, some hints and cautions:

The abbreviated state and province names given for the range of a plant indicate, in most instances, the corners or outer bounds of the area in which the plant grows as a native. They will usually begin at the northeastern corner and move clockwise back to the point of origin.

Zone numbers given here for trees, shrubs, and woody vines indicate approximately how far north the plant is winter hardy. They correspond to the zones on *Taylor's Encyclopedia of Gardening*'s plant hardiness map (see endpapers). The ability of plants to grow in any particular area is a combination of several factors, one of the most critical of which is their ability to survive the average minimum temperature of the coldest months. The zoning system is designed to show the hardiness of woody plants across the continent, and is based on weather records kept over a long period. Many plants, of course, have proved hardy outside their natural range.

Williamsburg lies in zone 6. March 25 is the average last killing spring frost date; April 26 the latest known. The earliest average fall frost date comes in the first week of November; mid-October is the earliest recorded. Average rainfall is 44 inches per year; during the growing season, the heaviest rainfall usually occurs in July and August. Flowering dates given are those for tidewater Virginia.

TREES

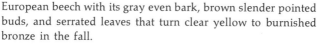

BEECH, AMERICAN
Fagus grandifolia Chrh.
Beech family (Fagaceae)

The American beech is a forest
tree that grows to a height of
100–120 feet. It resembles the
European beech with its gray even bark, brown slender pointed
buds, and serrated leaves that turn clear yellow to burnished
bronze in the fall.

The colonial woodworker occasionally found a use for beech
wood in making furniture and small household products. But it
was not a great utility hardwood as was the European beech in
the Old World; the colonists found several other hardwood
trees that served them better. Man, beast, and bird have eaten
the brown 3-angled nut. Hoards of passenger pigeons used to
come in the fall to the great beech forests of Kentucky to feed
on the litter of beechnuts beneath the trees. Cutting one's name
into the smooth bark of beech boles is a custom as old as
history. Young Englishmen of Shakespeare's day inscribed their
verses on the beech, as did young Romans before them. Daniel
Boone recorded on a beech tree that he had killed a bear in
Tennessee in 1760, and the scars of that incision were still
visible when the tree, estimated by the Forest Service to be 365
years old, fell in 1916.

"Beech" is derived from the ancient Anglo-Saxon and Gothic
in a close kinship with "book," thin boards of beech having
been used in the early period as a writing surface. *Grandifolia*
means "large foliage."

Native range: N. B. and Ont. to Fla. and Tex. Zone 3.

BLACK GUM

(black tupelo, sour gum)
Nyssa sylvatica Marsh.
Nyssa family (Nyssaceae)

Black gum grows up to 100 feet
tall and has a mastlike trunk
with gray to brown bark
somewhat like alligator leather. It produces small, sour fruits
but no gum, and often grows in association with sweet gums. In
autumn the leaves turn a brilliant yellow red, and, at the last,
dark wine red.

"Tupelo" may come from the Creek Indian *eto*, "tree," and
opelwv, "swamp," as the tree closely resembles tupelo gum or
water tupelo (*N. aquatica*), which grows in wet places and in
swamps. *Nyssa* was the name of a water nymph in classical
mythology; *sylvatica* means "forest."

Native range: Me. to Fla.
and Tex. Zone 3.

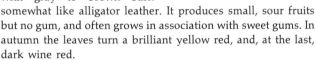

BUCKEYE, RED

Aesculus pavia L.
Buckeye or Horsechestnut
family (Hippocastanaceae)

The red buckeye, called by
John Bartram the "Scarlet
flowering Horse Chestnut," is
one of the showiest of the buckeyes, and was introduced into
England about 1711. A tree 15 to 20 feet tall, its upright panicles
of bell-shaped red flowers open in April and May. Roots and
bark yielded a gummy substance that was sometimes used as a
substitute for soap in washing clothes.

"Buckeye" is the name given to the American species of shrubs and trees of the Horsechestnut family because early Americans saw in the smooth, chestnut-colored nut with its long pale scar a resemblance to the eye of a deer. Most buckeyes have 5, instead of the horsechestnuts' 7, palmately arranged leaflets, and most have a smooth outer nutcase as compared to the prickly outer case of horsechestnuts.

Aesculus is an old Latin name for a tree, probably an oak; *pavia* for Peter Paaw, Dutch professor of botany at Leyden. Native range: N. C. and Tenn. to Fla. and La. Zone 4.

Yellow or sweet buckeye (*A. octandra* Marsh.), native from Pennsylvania to Georgia and Illinois, is one of the most beautiful of the buckeyes and may attain 90 feet. It resembles a horsechestnut in stature and aspect more closely than other buckeyes.

CATALPA
Catalpa bignonioides Walt.
Bignonia family
(Bignoniaceae)

This medium-sized tree, 20 to 60 feet high, is not particularly shapely, but it does have its great moments. In May and June the many flowered pyramidal panicles appear all white, but each flower, somewhat like an orchid, is yellow striped and on the inside is spotted chocolate brown. In the fall, when the large light green leaves turn a clear Chinese yellow and the long thin green dangling seedpods are seen against a sunlit October sky, the tree takes on a pagoda-like appearance.

Mark Catesby discovered the catalpa and introduced it into England in 1726. There is some evidence that this was the tree chosen to enhance "the Avenue to the Governor's House" in 1737. In his plan of the Palace about 1779, Jefferson noted "the rows of trees 100 f. apart," but did not say what they were. However, the translator of a manuscript journal kept by General de Lauberdière gives this entry for July 1782: "The Governor of Virginia also had in Williamsburg a very fine palace, built at the extremity of a handsome street planted with catalpas." Catalpa trees were planted 100 feet apart across Palace Green in the course of restoration after 1930.

"Catalpa" is the latinized form of the Cherokee Indian name. Other common names are cigar tree and Indian-bean tree. Bignonioides, "bignonialike," refers to the resemblance of the flowers to those of other members of the Bignonia family.

Native range: Ga. to Fla. and Miss. and naturalized further north. Zone 3.

CHERRY, BLACK
Prunus serotina Ehrh.
Rose family (Rosaceae)

On favorable sites the wild black cherry may grow to be a lofty tree, attaining 100 feet, the tallest of all the cherries. It is more familiar, though, as a smaller tree of relatively recently disturbed places—fence rows, old pastures, and old fields—than as a major forest tree. The white blossoms open when the leaves are partially grown, the fruit ripening in late summer and autumn. Appalachian mountain men pressed the fruit and infused it in brandy or rum to make the cordial, "cherry bounce." Bears take their cherries straight, the cubs following their mothers up the trees.

The wood of the wild black cherry is smooth grained and is for the cabinetmaker one of the choicest of all native woods. He ranks it second only to the wood of the black walnut.

Native range: N. S. to Fla., Tex., and N. D.; also west to Ariz. and below the border through Mex. to Guatemala. Zone 1.

[16]

CHERRY-LAUREL

Prunus caroliniana Ait.
(syn. *Laurocerasus
caroliniana* Mill. Roemer)
Rose family (Rosaceae)

The American cherry-laurel is
an evergreen tree growing 20 to
40 feet high. The glossy leaves
are slightly toothed, and the minute cream white flowers, in
dense axillary racemes, are followed by small shiny black
berries.

Cherry-laurel is also called laurel-cherry; in fact, *Laurocerasus*
is the Latin for "laurel-cherry."

Native range: N. C. to Tex., mostly near the coast. Zone 6.

COTTONWOOD, EASTERN

Populus deltoides Marsh.
Willow family (Salicaceae)

This poplar, attaining a height
of some 100 feet, is one of the
fastest growing trees. The
flowers are borne in catkins 3–4 inches long that appear before
the leaves, and the seeds are expelled on the wind in drifts of
downy white fluff—hence the name "cottonwood" for the
American species. Like the bigtooth aspen, the petioles of the
leaves of the cottonwood are flattened near the juncture with
the blade, resulting in the peculiar flutter of the leaves in the
wind.

Native range: Que. to Fla., Tex., and N. D. Zone 2.

[17]

CRAPE MYRTLE

Lagerstroemia indica L.
Loosestrife family (Lythraceae)

This multiple-stemmed shrub or tree, up to 20–30 feet tall, is often called "Lilac of the South" and is one of the most showy midsummer flowering trees in cultivation. It is easily identified the year round by its smooth, white to buff, flaking bark. The flowers—white, red, or lavender—are most commonly pink, frilled or crinkled like crepe paper, and are borne in dense clusters 4–9 inches long from the end of June to September. In the fall the leaves blaze orange gold to scarlet.

Crape myrtle, native to China and long cultivated in India, reached Europe by 1759. It is generally believed that André Michaux brought the tree to the South. Washington received specimens from the East Indies in 1799.

The genus name commemorates Magnus von Lagerstroem of Sweden; *indica,* India.

Widely grown in Williamsburg and throughout the South. Zone 5.

THE DOGWOODS

Cornus
Dogwood family (Cornaceae)

There are about 40 species of dogwood—deciduous (rarely evergreen) trees, shrubs, or low herbs—mostly scattered over the northern hemisphere. "Dogwood," the common name applied to some species, may originate from Parkinson's opinion that the fruit of the European *Cornus mas* was "not fit to be eaten, or to be given to a dogge." Or the name may come from "dagwood," since in Europe the wood, which is as hard as horn, was used in making daggers and meat skewers. *Cornus* means "horn."

CORNELIAN CHERRY
C. mas L.

This European shrub or small
tree grows up to 25 feet tall. In
early spring the naked twigs
are crowded with balls or heads of minute yellow flowers.
Brought to England from Austria in the late 1500s, the cornelian
cherry was introduced into Dutch New Amsterdam from Holland in 1642 by Adrian Van der Donke—Yonkers was named
for him. In England, gardeners grew it in the orchard or fruit
garden for its acid, carnelian colored, cherrylike berries that
ripen in August.

The specific name *mas*, "Male," was applied because the tree
produces flowers only until some 20–30 years old.

Zone 3.

FLOWERING DOGWOOD
C. florida L.

Flowering dogwood, the state
flower of Virginia, is a small
tree 10–20 feet in height and is a
fine ornamental the year round.
In winter gray button-shaped
flower buds stud the bare branches. In April–May the true
flowers bloom in a yellowish pincushionlike cluster at the base

of 4 notched, petallike, white or rosy pink bracts with a pinch or twist at the tip.

Dogwood is a prime wood on account of its hardness and shock-resistant quality: strong, light, wearing smooth with use, tool handles, maul and mallet heads, and weavers' shuttles were made of it. Even up to the end of the nineteenth century, many a toothbrush was made from the frayed twigs. William Byrd II considered the bark a preventive against malaria. In his *Histories of the Dividing Line betwixt Virginia and North Carolina* Byrd wrote, "Our chief medicine was Dogwood bark, which we used instead of that of Peru."

Catesby illustrated this dogwood in his *Natural History* and discovered the pink form. "In *Virginia* I found one of these Dogwood Trees with flowers of a rose-colour, which was luckily blown down, and many of the Branches had taken Root, which I transplanted into a Garden," probably that of Custis, because Catesby planted three pink dogwoods there.

Native range: Me. to Fla., Mex., and Kans. Zone 4.

ELM, AMERICAN
Ulmus americana L.
Elm family (Ulmaceae)

The American elm may be called the landscape painter's tree. Sometimes oaklike in form, with heavy, horizontal branches, sometimes "weeping" or "feathered," American elm's most characteristic form is fountainlike or vase-shaped. At about one-third of its height, the main trunk separates into several symmetrically equal branches. These soar upward, gradually arching outward as they mount to form a dome with down-pointing, drooping branchlets.

It is said that the elm, more than any other tree, has been

planted purely for the sake of its beauty along the streets and around the squares of American towns. But the tree has long been prey to serious pests; one, the elm bark beetle, is a carrier of a fungus disease known as Dutch elm disease, most prevalent in the northeast and the midwest. Many a town and village is now utterly devoid of its elms, but a number still grow in the Historic Area in Williamsburg.

Native range: formerly Nfld. to Fla. and west to the base of the Rocky Mts. Zone 2.

FIG, COMMON
Ficus carica L.
Mulberry family (Moraceae)

The common fig is a small, soft-wooded, and heavily branched shrub or tree up to 30 feet in height. The leaves are thick, usually deeply 3–5-lobed, and 4–8 inches long; rough above and downy beneath. The flowers bloom and mature within the pear-shaped syncarp or "fruit," which never opens.

Native to the Mediterranean region, the fig is one of the oldest fruits in cultivation. It was brought to the American colonies early. A Mrs. Pearce of Jamestown recorded in 1629 that one year she had obtained 100 bushels of figs from her 3- to 4-acre garden. Thomas Glover, in his *Account of Virginia* published in the Royal Society's *Philosophical Transactions,* June 20, 1676, observed that "good figs" were grown on the plantations. Philip Vickers Fithian, tutor at Nomini Hall, Robert Carter's plantation, wrote in his diary on August 26, 1774: "We gathered some Figs, the Ladies seem fond of them, I cannot endure them."

Ficus is the old Latin name; *carica* for Caria in Asia Minor. Zone 6.

GOLDENRAIN TREE

Koelreuteria paniculata Laxm.
Soapberry family
(Sapindaceae)

This oriental from Korea,
China, and Japan grows up to
30 feet tall. It has handsome
compound leaves and in July–August bears large panicles of
yellow flowers. The papery-walled seedpods eventually turn
from green to brown. The tree was named for Joseph G.
Koelreuter, professor of natural history in Karlsruhe, Germany.
Zone 3.

The goldenrain tree is sometimes mistaken for golden chain
or laburnum (*Laburnum anagyroides* Medic.). This large shrub or
small tree with erect or spreading branches, often close to the
ground, blooms in May and June. Its yellow-keeled flowers are
borne in pendulous racemes about 10 inches long. John Custis
said that his laburnums grew into "pretty Large Trees." Native
to southern Europe, the laburnum was introduced into England in 1560 and belongs to the bean family (Fabaceae
[Leguminosae]).

HACKBERRY

Celtis laevigata Willd.
Elm family (Ulmaceae)

This wide, broad-headed tree
with more or less pendulous
branches grows up to 100 feet.

It was not an easy tree for early naturalists to identify because the leaves are like those of a nettle rather than those of any other tree. The southern species was called the "unknown wood," and the northern species (*C. occidentalis*) the "unknown tree." The small berrylike fruits, about a quarter of an inch across, are orange red. When ripe, they turn dark purple and exude a sweet, sticky substance that accounts for the common name sugarberry. In wintertime the hackberry reveals itself as the twiggiest of trees.

Surveyors of the Virginia–North Carolina Dividing Line used hackberry trees as boundary markers. Peter Collinson grew both American hackberries, and, as he wrote John Bartram, one of them came from Virginia. There is an outstandingly large sugarberry in the Robert Carter House garden in Williamsburg.

"Hackberry" is the debased form of hedgeberry. *Celtis* is an ancient Greek name, perhaps for the hackberry, *C. australis*, of southern Europe; *laevigata* means "smooth."

Native range: Coastal Va. to Fla. and eastern Tex. Zone 3.

HICKORY, MOCKERNUT
(white or whiteheart hickory)
Carya tomentosa (Poir.) Nutt.
Walnut family (Juglandaceae)

Given room enough, mocker-nut grows into a magnificent tree, up to 100 feet. The leaves are resinous and fragrant and, as with all hickories, turn a soft, dull, rich yellow in the fall. In his *Historie of Travaile into Virginia Britannia* (1640), William Strachey describes it growing in the Tidewater. There is evidence that the colonists grew it for its beauty as well as for the sweet, light brown nut.

"Hickory" is from an Indian word; *Carya* is the Greek for "walnut"; *tomentosa* means "woolly."

Native range: Mass. to Nebr., Fla., and Tex. Zone 4.

THE HOLLIES
Ilex
Holly family (Aquifoliaceae)

The folklore and legends about hollies as a group are innumerable. Above all, holly is symbolic of Christmas. Opinions differ as to whether the name is a corruption of "holy" (William Turner called the tree "Holy" and "Holytree"), or whether it stems from *holgen*, the Anglo-Saxon name for the English holly. Confusingly, the genus name is also the specific name of *Quercus ilex*, the holm oak. The majority of the 300 evergreen and deciduous species are found in North and South America and tropical and temperate Asia; there are a few in Africa, Australia, and Europe.

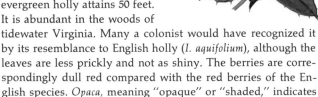

AMERICAN HOLLY
I. opaca Ait.

This slow growing, long-lived evergreen holly attains 50 feet. It is abundant in the woods of tidewater Virginia. Many a colonist would have recognized it by its resemblance to English holly (*I. aquifolium*), although the leaves are less prickly and not as shiny. The berries are correspondingly dull red compared with the red berries of the English species. *Opaca,* meaning "opaque" or "shaded," indicates these differences.

Washington and other colonial gardeners brought in young trees from the woods or raised them from berries. On March 28, 1786, Washington received some small holly trees boxed in earth from Colonel "Lighthorse Harry" Lee (father of Robert E. Lee). He set them out in his holly planting semicircle at Mount Vernon. Fifteen years earlier Jefferson had thought of enclosing a burial ground with either a "stone wall with a holly hedge on it," or with red cedar trees.

Holly is an ideal wood for inlay work, approaching ivory in color. It was used, along with boxwood, for the inlay work on the staircase in the rebuilt Governor's Palace in Williamsburg.

Native range: Mass. to Fla., west to Mo. and Tex. Zone 4.

POSSUMHAW

I. decidua Walt.

Known also as swamp holly, this deciduous holly is a large shrub or small tree some 25 feet tall with grayish twigs and branches. The berries, in small clusters, turn bright orange to red in the fall and remain on the tree until early the following spring.

Native range: Md. to Fla., Tex., and Mo. Zone 5.

WINTERBERRY

I. verticillata (L.) Gray

This deciduous shrub grows up to 10 feet. Bunched along the stem, the berries turn a vivid red in October, and, usually left alone by the birds, persist until midwinter. The specific name describes the vertical whorl or circle of berries around the stem.

Native range: Can. to Fla., west to Wis. and Mo. Zone 3.

YAUPON HOLLY
I. vomitoria Ait.

Yaupon is a much branched
evergreen shrub up to 25 feet
that grows quickly and vigor-
ously. The small scarlet and somewhat translucent berries ripen
in the fall. Dr. Alexander Garden of Charleston found that "it
makes a very good and most beautiful hedge and may be kept
as short and neat as Box." As John Lawson noted, "It grows the
most like Box of any vegetable that I know, being very like it in
Leaf, only dented exactly like Tea, but the Leaf somewhat
fatter." Yaupon holly is widely used for both hedges and
topiaries in the gardens of Colonial Williamsburg. Indians and
colonists made yaupon tea from the leaves and branches. It is a
far milder stimulant than the "black drink" the Indians in the
Deep South made from a mixture of various roots. Mark
Catesby compared yaupon tea with a drink made from
I. paraguayensis, traded by the Spaniards to Buenos Aires, South
America, which may be the drink now called *maté.* Yaupon tea
is still made in North Carolina.

Vomitoria refers to the plant's emetic qualities.

Native range: Va. to Fla., Tex., and Ark. Zone 6.

HORNBEAM, AMERICAN
(blue beech)
Carpinus caroliniana Walt.
Beech family (Fagaceae)

American hornbeam is an
understory forest tree that
grows up to 40 feet. With its

smoothly furrowed slate blue colored bark, the tree resembles the common hornbeam (*C. betulus*) of Britain and Europe; both species tend to retain their rich brown dead leaves through the winter. The leaves resemble those of the beech tree, hence American hornbeam is sometimes known as blue beech.

In England and in Europe, *C. betulus* has for centuries been used to make clipped hedges. John Evelyn described the admirable "Espalier-hedge" of the long middle walk at the Luxembourg Garden in Paris and the "Close-walk" at England's Hampton Court—both of hornbeam. Some of the hedges in the gardens of Colonial Williamsburg and some of the arbors, those shady summertime outdoor retreats, are of American hornbeam; the largest is in the Wythe garden.

"Hornbeam" refers to the hardness of the wood: "horn" for toughness, "beam" an old word for tree; another common name is ironwood. *Carpinus* is the old Latin name.

Native range: N. S. to Ont. and Minn., south to Fla. and Tex. Zone 3.

KENTUCKY COFFEE TREE

Gymnocladus dioica (L.) K. Koch
Bean family (Fabaceae [Leguminosae])

The Kentucky coffee tree is a large tree, 100 feet or more in height, branching near the ground into a few ascending limbs that form a narrow round-topped head. The leaves are twice-compound, the leaflets arranged feather-fashion in pairs. The pealike flowers, in clustered racemes, appear in May–June and are followed by flat green pods 4–10 inches long that contain large and flattened seeds.

To the early settlers, the Kentucky coffee tree was new and unfamiliar—it is one of but two species in the genus *Gymnocladus*, the other of which grows in central China. Settlers in Kentucky and Tennessee roasted coffee tree seeds instead of using the true coffee berry, and the white pulp of the green pod was used in medicines.

Gymnocladus is from the Greek for naked and branch, alluding to some of the branches being without twigs; *dioica* means dioecious, that is, having female flowers on one plant and male on the other.

Native range: Scattered through Del. to Va., Okla., and S. D. Zone 4.

THE LINDENS
Tilia
Linden family (Tiliaceae)

Some 30 species of linden or lime trees are native to the north temperate zone. Their flowers secrete an abundance of nectar, and bees throng to the fragrant flowers. The tree's sapwood is so soft and light that honeycomb is framed in it. On entering the church, the father of Linnaeus changed his name to Linné for love of a linden tree in his garden.

Lime is simply another version of the Anglo-Saxon linden; *Til-ia* is the classical Latin name.

AMERICAN LINDEN
(basswood, lime)
T. americana L.

The American linden reaches 120 feet in height and makes a fine round-headed shade tree. The leaves, coarsely serrated, are 4–6 inches long. In June bees throng to the panicles of yellowish white fragrant flowers suspended on threadlike stems from the bracts above.

[28]

The Iroquois used the cortex of the bark in ropemaking, hence the name "basswood."

Native range: Que. to Ala., Tex., and Man.

SMALL-LEAVED LINDEN
T. cordata Mill.

Small-leaved linden is native to Europe and is the only species native to Britain. The tree reaches 100 feet in height and is very similar, although smaller in all its parts, to the American species. The roundish-oval glossy green leaves are $1\frac{1}{2}$ to 3 inches long and wide. The soft smooth wood was used by English woodcarvers, notably by Grinling Gibbons (1648–1720), who is famous for his ornamental carving of birds, flowers, foliage, and fruits. John Evelyn recommended Gibbons to Charles II, who employed him, as did the famous architect, Sir Christopher Wren.

Cordata, meaning heart-shaped, refers to the leaves.
Zone 3.

THE LOCUSTS
Robinia and *Gleditsia*
Bean family (Fabaceae [Leguminosae])

BLACK LOCUST
(false acacia)
R. pseudo-acacia L.

Black locust grows up to 80 feet. There are 7–12 leaflets to each compound leaf. The so-called "sleep" of the leaves occurs at nightfall when the leaflets droop on their stalks, seeming to fold up for the night. In June clusters of white, beanlike, honey-scented flowers hang down in 4–8-inch-long racemes (like those of the white wisteria). The conspicuous seed pods are about 4 inches long.

William Strachey wrote in 1610 about "a kynd of low tree, which bears a pod like to the peas, but nothing so big; we take that to be locust." Some Jamestown settlers were surprisingly knowledgeable about plants. One or more must have known of the "locust" tree of southern Europe, the carob tree (*Ceratonia silique*), to which the name of the noisy insect was attached on account of the tree's rattling, sweet, edible pods. However, the carob only grows—indifferently—in the southernmost part of England. Perhaps the tree was familiar from illustrations, as the seeds were the original "carat" weight of London goldsmiths. Or perhaps there was a botanist able to observe that black locust belongs, as does the carob, to the Fabaceae (Leguminosae) family.

Black locust wood is extremely durable in contact with the soil, as Catesby testified. He went to Jamestown a little over a century after its founding and observed: "Being obliged to run up with all the expedition possible such little houses as might serve them to dwell in, til they could find leisure to build larger and more convenient ones, they erected each of their little hovels on four only of these trees [the Locust-tree of Virginia], pitched into the ground to support the four corners; many of these posts are yet standing, and not only the parts underground, but likewise, those above, still perfectly sound."

Captain William Fitzhugh of Virginia considered the wood "as durable as most brick walls" and used locust fencing to enclose his orchard. When Philadelphia was founded in the 1680s, the chief streets were named after trees—one was Locust Street.

Locusta is the Latin for locust. The genus name commemorates Jean Robin and his son Vespasian, both of whom were appointed herbalists to Henry IV of France. *Pseudo-acacia* refers to the similarity of the feathery foliage with that of the acacia. Black locust is sometimes known as honey locust for its fragrant flowers, but the common name "honey locust" is usually applied to *Gleditsia triacanthos* because of its sweet-tasting pod.

Native range: Pa. to Ga., west to La. and Okla. Zone 3.

HONEY LOCUST
(sweet locust, three-
thorned acacia)
G. triacanthos L.

Honey locust reaches 140 feet
in height. It has compound
leaves. The scentless flowers,
in April–May, are less noticeable than the succeeding pods,
which are flat, slightly twisted, and up to a foot long. A sweetish
pulp around each seed and the triple-branched thorns account
for the common names. The thorns were once used in carding
wool and pinning up woolsacks, but a thornless form is now
commonly planted. Mark Catesby described and illustrated the
honey locust in his *Natural History.*

    Gleditsia is from J. Gottlieb Gleditsch (1714–1786), director of
the Berlin botanic garden; *triacanthos* is the Greek for "three-
thorned."

    Native range: N. Y. to Fla., Tex., and S. D. Zone 3.

THE MAGNOLIAS
Magnolia
Magnolia family (Magnoliaceae)

This genus of 80 species of trees includes some of the most
beautiful of flowering trees, unrivaled in the size of their flowers. Magnolias are found in the wild in North and Central
America, eastern Asia, and the Himalayas. Some are evergreen,
some deciduous. Sweet bay magnolia was the first American
species introduced into England, being among the plants sent
by John Banister to Bishop Henry Compton in 1688. Linnaeus
chose the name "magnolia" to honor Pierre Magnol (1638–
1715), who was director of the botanic garden at Montpellier,

France, because "it is handsome both in foliage and flower and worthy of so fine a man."

SOUTHERN MAGNOLIA
(bull bay)
M. grandiflora L.

This is the great ornamental tree of the southern states, an evergreen attaining 100 feet. Its leaves are oval but tapered to both ends, 6–10 inches long, a lustrous dark green above, rusty-felted beneath. The goblet-shaped flowers, 7–8 inches across, are ivory white and heavily fragrant. June is the peak flowering month in Williamsburg, although a few flowers appear throughout the summer months up to Thanksgiving. In October the seed cones turn rosy red, soon opening as woody structures studded with scarlet seeds.

In 1757 Dr. Alexander Garden declared this magnolia to be "the finest and most superb evergreen tree that this earth produced." Mark Catesby referred to *M. grandiflora* as "M. altissima, the Laurel Tree of Carolina." Georg Dionysius Ehret, the great botanical artist, made the drawing for the colored engraving of *M. grandiflora* in Catesby's *Natural History.*

Native range: Southeastern Va. to Fla., Ark., and Tex. Zone 5.

SWEET BAY MAGNOLIA
M. virginiana L.

Sweet bay stays evergreen and reaches 60 feet in the South. The northern form is deciduous and often shrublike. It is not as spectacular as many magnolias; its slender, green leaves are coated with a whitish film on the underside, and the flowers, white and 2–3 inches across, first open in May and continue in succession over the summer months. Although there are not enough blooms at any one time to make a display, their fragrance is unmatched and more pervasive than that of the southern magnolia. Robert Beverley concluded that the fragrance of the Virginia woods came from "the fine tulip-bearing Laurel-Tree which has the pleasantest Smell in the World, and keeps Blossoming and Seeding several months together."

Other names are swamp laurel, swamp magnolia, and beaver tree. Beaver traps were baited with the bark and the root since beavers like sweet bay as much as mice do cheese. Peter Kalm said a traveler knew when he was in beaver tree country because the scent of its blossoms carried "within three quarters of an English mile—provided the wind was not against it. The whole air is filled with their sweet and pleasant scent."

Native range: Pa. and N. J. to Fla., Miss., and Tenn. Zone 3.

The red bay (*Persea borbonia*), an evergreen tree related to the avocado, is sometimes mistaken for the sweet bay magnolia; they often grow in association along streams and borders of swamps. Red bay has bright green lustrous leaves coated with a waxy bloom on the underside. The inconspicuous flowers are followed by a small black fruit.

UMBRELLA MAGNOLIA
(umbrella tree)
M. tripetala L.

The umbrella tree is a large shrub or small tree that rarely grows over 35 feet tall. Its leaves are unusually large—10–20 inches long—and are clustered near the tip of the twigs, giving an open umbrellalike effect. The cup-shaped, ill-scented, cream colored flowers, with 6–9 petals, are 6–10 inches across, appear with the leaves, and are followed by the seedcones that become rose colored in the fall.

Tripetala refers to the 3 larger, more erect uppermost petals.

Native range: Pa. to Ala. and west to Ark. and Mo. Zone 3.

THE MAPLES
Acer
Maple family (Aceraceae)

Maples are widely distributed in North America, Europe, and parts of Asia and North Africa. The sugar, red, and silver maples, each attaining a height of 120 feet, are the leaders among American species. *Acer* is the classical Latin name.

RED MAPLE
(scarlet, swamp)
A. rubrum L.

There is something red about this maple at all times of the year; even the winter buds and the leaf stems are red. The long-stalked, scarlet vermilion flowers open in early spring long before the leaves, giving the whole tree a gauzy red appearance. The leaves are 3–5-lobed, usually 3, the lobes forming a V-angle, and turn crimson in the fall.

Native range: Nfld. and Gaspé Pen., Que., to Man., south to Mex. and beyond. Zone 2.

SILVER MAPLE

A. saccharinum L.

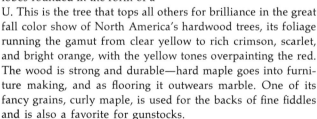

The leaves of the silver maple are 5-lobed, sharply toothed, deeply cut, and silvery white on the underside. The beauty of the tree lies in the grace and suppleness with which the leaves respond to every breath of wind. One moment the tree is all green, the next all silver.

Native range: N. B. to Ont. and Minn.; south to Mex. and beyond. Zone 2.

SUGAR MAPLE

A. saccharum Marsh.

Sugar maple leaves are 5-lobed, the angles between the lobes rounded in the form of a U. This is the tree that tops all others for brilliance in the great fall color show of North America's hardwood trees, its foliage running the gamut from clear yellow to rich crimson, scarlet, and bright orange, with the yellow tones overpainting the red. The wood is strong and durable—hard maple goes into furniture making, and as flooring it outwears marble. One of its fancy grains, curly maple, is used for the backs of fine fiddles and is also a favorite for gunstocks.

Captain John Smith was the first to describe how the New England Indians made sugar from the sap. Maple furniture, maple sugar, maple syrup, and maple flavoring have long since become American household words.

Native range: Que. to Man., Tex., and Ga. Zone 2.

MEDLAR

Mespilus germanica L.
Rose family (Rosaceae)

The medlar is a slender and somewhat crooked growing tree up to 25 feet tall. The flowers are white and solitary. The fruits are distinctive: an inch wide, flattish, apple-shaped, and crinkly on top. They take form early, soon turning from green to russet brown, and adorn the tree for several months. Medlars are best after the first frosts, and are not fit to use until ripe-rotten. Being rich in pectin, they were used in jelly making.

Native to southeastern Europe and Persia, the tree is often seen in old English gardens but rarely in North America, although there are several in Colonial Williamsburg. "Medlar" is named for the botanist Medicus who created a new genus for the tree in 1789; *mespilus* is the old Latin name.

Zone 3.

THE MULBERRIES

Morus
Mulberry family (Moraceae)

Morus is a genus of some 12 species of deciduous trees and shrubs native to North America and Asia. Some species are grown for the edible fruits, others for the leaves on which silkworms feed. "Mulberry" stems from murberry or morberry, a combination of *morus,* the old Latin name, and "berry."

RED MULBERRY
M. rubra L.

This native species grows up to
60–70 feet and is the largest of
the mulberries. At first the col-
onists believed it to be a variety of *M. alba,* cultivated in Asia
and Europe for silk culture, and referred to it as white mulberry
in early correspondence. The abundance of the native tree in
the Tidewater gave rise to hopes for silk culture in the colony.
In 1619 the burgesses decreed that every man should plant and
tend 6 trees a year for 7 years; later, bounties of so much
tobacco for so much silk were offered, and penalties were
threatened for failure to plant. Eventually the red mulberry was
recognized as different from either the white or the black
mulberry (*M. nigra*), both of which were imported. (*M. nigra,*
also called English mulberry, is native to western Asia and was
also cultivated for centuries in many countries for its dark red,
sweet fruits and for silk culture.) By the mid-seventeenth century various types of mulberries were so much a part of the
Tidewater scene that the trees were used in and around Jamestown as boundary markers.

The red mulberry's bark was also said to make a "good linen
cloth and Cordage." Le Page du Pratz said in his *History of
Louisiana* that many of the Choctaw women "wear cloaks of the
bark of the mulberry tree, or of the feathers of swans, turkies,
or India ducks." Tidewater Indians ate quantities of the dark
purple berries; the colonists used them sparsely and mostly fed
them to poultry and hogs.

Native range: Vt. to Fla., Tex., and Minn.

WHITE MULBERRY
M. alba L.

The white mulberry, native to
China, has white or pinkish
insipid tasting fruits, but for
centuries it was cultivated in its homeland and in southern
Europe for its leaves, from which the silkworm makes the finest
and most highly prized silk. Edward Digges, governor of the
Virginia colony 1655–1656, raised silkworms, and in 1658 presented Charles II with a sample of silk produced by a fellow
planter, Colonel Thomas Pettus, on his plantation, Littletown,
adjacent to Kingsmill on the James River. Governor Sir William
Berkeley ordered further planting of white mulberry trees, and
one Gloucester County landowner planted 70,000 in 1664–1665.
The burgesses earmarked his bounty as 20,000 pounds of
tobacco. But silk culture in the Virginia colony never came up
to expectations, and toward the close of the seventeenth century
attempts to establish it ended.

Zone 3.

PAPER MULBERRY
Broussonetia papyrifera (L.) Vent.

Although the paper mulberry
is included in the mulberry
family, it is not a true mul-
berry. Being a dioecious plant—male and female flowers borne

on separate plants—the male trees bear no fruit. The leaves are lobed like those of the sassafras and 3–8 inches long; silkworms have no interest in them. The grayish trunks of older trees are gnarled and knotted, and the tree takes on an aged and somewhat grotesque appearance.

Paper mulberry is native to Burma, China, and Polynesia, and is widely cultivated in Japan, where the inner bark is used for papermaking and in making paper lanterns and umbrellas. For centuries the bark has been used in the Pacific for making tapa cloth.

In 1751 the seed was brought to Peter Collinson from China. Its introduction into North America is associated with André Michaux, since it was among the plants he brought with him in 1785. There is, however, a reference to its introduction from Europe in 1784 by William Hamilton of Woodlands near Philadelphia. From time to time Jefferson planted several paper mulberries; there were 64 in the nursery at Monticello in 1816. He valued the trees "for the regularity of their form, velvet leaf and for being fruitless. They are charming near a porch for densely shading it."

Broussonetia in honor of Pierre Broussonet, French naturalist and botanist; *papyrifera* means paper-providing.

Zone 4.

THE OAKS
Quercus
Beech Family (Fagaceae)

There are over 600 species of oak trees or shrubs, evergreen or deciduous, distributed over the subtropical and temperate regions of the northern hemisphere, more than 20 of which are native to Virginia. The common name is derived from the Anglo-Saxon *ac; quercus* is the Latin name for the oak tree.

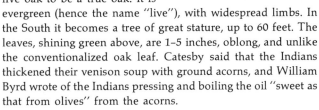

LIVE OAK
Q. virginiana Mill.

Small acorns, borne in clusters
about 1 inch long, proclaim the
live oak to be a true oak. It is
evergreen (hence the name "live"), with widespread limbs. In
the South it becomes a tree of great stature, up to 60 feet. The
leaves, shining green above, are 1–5 inches, oblong, and unlike
the conventionalized oak leaf. Catesby said that the Indians
thickened their venison soup with ground acorns, and William
Byrd wrote of the Indians pressing and boiling the oil "sweet as
that from olives" from the acorns.

Native range: Va. to Fla.,
Mex., and Okla. Zone 6.

SCARLET OAK
Q. coccinea Muenchh.

Since colonial days the scarlet
oak has been recognized as a
splendid ornamental. Some 80
feet in height, in autumn the light green, shiny, sharply serrated
leaves turn a brilliant scarlet (hence *coccinea*). Bartram greatly
admired this tree, often remarking upon it in his journal. In
1691 this lovely tree reached England.

Native range: Me. to Fla., Minn., and Mo. Zone 2.

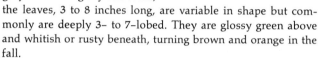

SOUTHERN RED OAK

(Spanish oak)

Q. falcata Michaux

Southern red oak reaches a
height of 80 to 100 feet. The
gray bark is slightly furrowed;
the leaves, 3 to 8 inches long, are variable in shape but commonly are deeply 3- to 7-lobed. They are glossy green above and whitish or rusty beneath, turning brown and orange in the fall.

There seems no satisfactory answer as to why this oak was called "Spanish" oak, but that was the name William Penn and William Byrd II knew it by. *Falcata* comes from falco, a falcon, the sickle-shaped leaves being likened to a falcon's curved talons.

Native range: Vt. to Fla., Tex.,
Nebr., and Minn. Zone 3.

WHITE OAK

Q. alba L.

Of all North America's oak
trees, the white oak is closest
to the English oak. It is a
broad-crowned tree that reaches a girth of 20 feet and a height of 100–150 feet. The 5–9-lobed leaves have a whitish bloom on the underside; on younger trees the dead russet leaves stay on all winter.

The large acorn was a staple food for the Indians, and some colonists rubbed themselves with the oil they extracted to help them "supple their joynts." Peter Kalm said that the bark "was reckoned the best remedy which had yet been found against the dysentery." It was also used in tanning leather and in ship-building and pipemaking—a "pipe" being a cask for wine and other liquids. Staves of white oak were sent to France and to the West Indies to be made into casks for wine and rum. It is the best all-around fireplace wood.

"White" oak is named for the light gray or nearly white bark; *alba*, from the Latin "white."

Native range: Me. to Fla., Minn., and Tex. Zone 2.

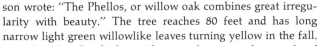

WILLOW OAK
Q. phellos L.

In colonial days the willow oak was regarded as "a strong and comely tree." Thomas Jeffer-son wrote: "The Phellos, or willow oak combines great irregu-larity with beauty." The tree reaches 80 feet and has long narrow light green willowlike leaves turning yellow in the fall.

Phellos, the Greek for cork, was the name for a related species, the cork oak (*Q. suber*).

Native range: N. J. to Fla., Tex., Okla., and Mo. Zone 4.

PAWPAW
(custard-apple)
Asimina triloba (L.) Dunal
Custard-Apple family
(Annonaceae)

Pawpaw is a small, unusual tree that Catesby included in his *Natural History*. The leaves,

10–12 inches long and 4–6 inches across, are light green, paler on the undersides; the flowers, green at first, turn brown and then, at the last, a dark wine color. The stubby bananalike fruit colors as it matures, the greenish yellow skin finally turning brown and becoming wrinkled; the flesh is custardy when ripe. William Byrd II said that "all sorts of good things, likewise sweetmeats" were made with it. In 1737 Peter Collinson asked John Bartram to send him flowers, seeds, and fruit preserved in rum. Bartram complied in December 1738 when he stopped at Williamsburg on the way home from one of his expeditions.

"Pawpaw" (also spelled papaw) is from the Spanish *papayo;* *Asimina* is from the Spanish *assimiar.*

Native range: N. J. to Fla., Tex., and Ont. Zone 1.

PECAN
Carya illinoensis
(Wang.) K. Koch
Walnut family (Juglandaceae)

This noble nut tree, North America's finest, attains 140–170 feet, with a trunk some-times 30 feet in girth, enormous limbs, and a spreading crown. The leaves, pinnately compound and 10–20 inches long, leaf out late in the spring when the flowers, in 3–5-inch catkins, dangle down in many flowered panicles. The nut is enclosed in a smooth, thin-skinned husk over 2 inches long.

The Spanish explorer Hernando de Soto and his men discovered the tree when they crossed the Mississippi in 1541. More than 200 years later, another traveler described the scene: "They [the trees] grow everywhere on the Banks of the Mississippi River from the Illinois River to the Sea." Carried eastward by traders and trappers, the nuts were first called Illinois nuts. The early writers of Louisiana reported that the Indians stored the nut, and by 1762 the Creoles were using it in the confection that became known as the praline.

Jefferson admired the tree and requested nuts from his friends to distribute at home and abroad. He "set great value on the chance of having a grove of them" at Monticello; in his diary for May 1786 he refers to a row of "Illinois nuts" he had just planted. St. George Tucker, who succeeded George Wythe as professor of law at the College of William and Mary, planted "six of the Illinois nuts brot. fr. Kentucky" at his home at Matoax, Virginia, in November 1787, the year before he moved to Williamsburg. He may have brought some pecan seedlings with him from Matoax or planted more nuts soon after his arrival, for a magnificent old pecan was still standing on the Tucker House property in 1976.

"Pecan" is from the Indian and Spanish name *paccan; Carya* is Greek for walnut.

Native range: Ind. to Ala., eastern Tex., and Iowa. Zone 4–Zone 6 for fruit.

PERSIMMON

Diospyros virginiana L.
Ebony family (Ebenaceae)

The persimmon, native in the South, is 40–60 feet tall, the first branches spreading out some 20 feet from the ground. The bole is straight and slender, the gray brown bark, broken into scaly blocks and separated by deep, narrow fissures, is not unlike alligator leather. Dark, almost tropical looking leaves hide the insignificant but fragrant flowers that are borne only on the female tree.

The fruit, a glaucous orange that turns deep tawny, is very astringent until fully ripe, as William Strachey learned at Jamestown: "When not fully ripe they are harsh and choakye, and furre a Mans mouth like Allam [alum], howbeit being taken fully ripe it is a reasonable pleasant fruiet somewhat lushious. I have seen our people put them into their baked and sodden puddings." Colonists also made persimmon beer and persimmon pudding, and the Indians used the juice and the dried pulp in their corncakes.

Persimmon belongs to the same genus as the ebony tree (*D. ebenun*), its heartwood so dark a brown as to be almost black. "Pasimenan" was one of the Indian names; *Diospyros* from the Greek *dios* and *pyron,* meaning "divine" and "grain" respectively. This reference to the fruit pertains to the fully ripe and much larger persimmon native to China and Japan, not to the Virginia species.

Native range: N. E. to Fla., Tex., and Kans. Zone 3.

THE PINES
Pinus
Pine family (Pinaceae)

There are about 80 species of these evergreen trees in the northern hemisphere, which are best identified by their needle-like leaves and cones. In the vicinity of Williamsburg only the 3 species here described are characteristic. *Pinus* is the classical Latin name.

LOBLOLLY PINE
P. taeda L.

Loblolly reaches over 100 feet, has 5–10-inch-long "needles" in bundles of 3, and 3–6-inch-long and narrowly conical cones. The almost black bark is divided on older trees into irregular dark brown scaly blocks. The Reverend John Clayton noticed that in the spring the pine's yellow pollen dust floated on the surface of the rainwater after heavy storms.

Loblolly grew widely in the southern coastal plains where the wood was used for its abundance and diversity. When aged, the wood was used for planking, shingles, posts, and sills. John Mitchell, who considered it the most useful of all the pines, called it the "light-wood" pine because when the tree dies, the heartwood often turns hard, and, being full of resin, will burn like a torch. Poor people used it instead of candles. A friend told Mitchell that when an old ship was broken up, its oak timbers were found to have rotted, but the loblolly was perfectly sound.

Loblolly has many common names, among them old-field pine (for the tree's habit of taking over abandoned worked-out land). One of the former meanings of the word "loblolly" was applied to a loutish person—"soft and useless." In the southern states the name "loblolly" was given to species found growing in soft, damp places such as the loblolly bay (*Gordonia lasianthus*), the loblolly magnolia (*M. grandiflora*), and the loblolly pine. *Taeda* means "loutish," "unattractive."

Native range: N. J. to Fla., Tex., and Okla. Zone 4.

SCRUB PINE
P. virginiana Mill.

Virginia scrub pine reaches 100 feet, has 1½–3-inch-long "needles" in clusters of 2, and 1½–2½-inch-long cones armed on the back with a slender prickle. The dark brown bark is separated by shallow fissures. This pine is a frequent companion of the loblolly and takes over abandoned fields as readily. It is chiefly used as good fuel.

Native range: N. Y. to Ga., Ark., and Ind. Zone 3.

WHITE PINE
P. strobus L.

White pine grows up to 150
feet and has 3–5-inch-long
slim bluish green "needles"
in bunches of 5 and narrowly oblong cones 4–8 inches long. The
bark becomes divided into roughly rectangular blocks by deep,
narrow fissures. This was once the predominant tree of the
north woods and occurs in the mountains well south of the
Mason-Dixon line.

It is said that white pine, more than any other American
forest tree, built the nation. It was used in frame houses for
boards, doors, window sashes, and shingles, and was the preferred wood for covered bridges. White pine was unrivaled as a
mastwood in shipbuilding. In the reign of William and Mary,
England's Navy Board decreed that the best pine masts be
reserved for the royal navy, and other decrees restricting its
exportation followed.

Native range: Nfld. to Iowa, Ga., and Man. Zone 2.

REDBUD

Cercis canadensis L.
Bean family (Fabaceae
[Leguminosae])

Redbud is a shrub or understory tree of the forest. Its
leaves are heart shaped. The

magenta colored pealike blossoms, in stalkless bunches, appear on the leafless branches and often on the trunks of older trees. Lawson said that North Carolinians used the blossoms in salads, and Kalm noted, while in Philadelphia, "cercis Canadensis, the Sallod Tree."

It is said that from this tree Judas Iscariot hanged himself, which is why the European species (*C. siliquastrum*) is known as the Judas tree. The name "redbud" for the American species was in use in North Carolina by 1700. *Cercis* comes from the Greek name, *kerkis*.

Native range: Conn., Fla., Mex., and Ont. Zone 3.

RED CEDAR, EASTERN
Juniperus virginiana L.
Cypress family
(Cupressaceae)

Eastern red cedar is an evergreen tree that grows up to 100 feet. On the eastern seaboard its form is spirelike in outline. The leaves in the young foliage are tiny sharp needles, and, in the mature foliage, tiny opposite scales. The "berries," actually fleshy cones, are pale green at first, then turn dark blue and are covered with a whitish bloom.

The eastern red cedar is not a true cedar, but a juniper. The name "cedar" is loosely applied to over 70 different kinds of trees, especially to species of juniper, for their cedarlike appearance or for the fragrance of their wood. The life span of the tree is, at most, 300 years. Many a Virginian once lined his way from road to house with it and used its wood for shingles and fences. Bluebirds nested in cedar fencepost holes.

The revised 1699 plans for the "Capitole, now erecting in the City of Williamsburg" specified that the porches be supported by cedar columns. John Bartram found William Byrd II "very prodigalle . . . in new Gates, gravel walk hedges and cedars finely turned . . . in short he hath the finest seat in Virginia." Later, pencilmakers found the clear, knot-free heartwood, light and easily sharpened, to be the best for their trade, and for nearly a century eastern red cedar supplied the world with pencil wood.

Juniperus is the old classical name.

Native range: Que. and Me. to Fla., Tex., and S. D. Zone 1.

SASSAFRAS

Sassafras albidum (Nutt.) Nees
Laurel family (Lauraceae)

Sassafras sometimes attains 80 feet in the South and has a thick, dark reddish brown bark covered by scales and ridges. Small clusters of yellowish flowers open on the naked wood in April and May. The leaves are simple, 2- or 3-lobed, and turn yellow orange to vermilion in the fall. The 2-lobed leaves resemble both right and left hand mittens—hence the colloquial name "mitten tree."

The Spanish in Florida, observing that the Indians used the bark of the root as a purifier and tonic and added the dried, powdered leaves to thicken their broth, named it "salsafras" (from saxifrage, supposed to have similar medicinal properties). The French Huguenots in South Carolina called it sassafras. In 1574 Dr. Nicholas Monardes, the Spanish physician, claimed the root bark was a cure-all. From then on, the dried root bark sold at a very high price in Europe, and explorers along North America's Atlantic coastline kept a sharp lookout for the tree, which became the oldest commercialized crop in North America.

Hariot, finding sassafras on Roanoke Island, described it as "a wood of the most sweet and pleasant smell and of rare virtues in medicine for the cure of many diseases." Jamestown lies in what was some of the best sassafras country in Virginia; sassafras was one of the first exports that Captain John Smith sent home from the settlement. Although the root bark's reputation diminished, faith in the blood purifying properties of sassafras tea has persisted, and the tea is now packaged and sold in tea bags. Sassafras is also used as a flavoring for root beer and candy sticks, and filé powder from the young leaves is an essential ingredient in gumbo dishes.

Albidum, "whitish," is believed to refer to the chalky undersides of the leaves.

Native range: Me. to Mich., south to Fla. and Tex. Zone 3.

SHADBUSH

Amelanchier canadensis
(L.) Medic.
Rose family (Rosaceae)

This is a small understory tree with light gray bark. Its finely petaled pure white flowers are borne on the leafless branches, usually appearing when the shad are running upriver to spawn—March or April in Virginia. The young leaves are covered with a silvery down and the small apple-shaped red or purple black fruits, ripening in June, were eaten by both Indians and colonists, and were used to flavor pies and hot breads. François Michaux noticed the berries on sale in the Philadelphia market and remarked that only children bought them.

Service, sarvis, sarvisberry, and Juneberry tree are other common names. Sarvis is the Elizabethan form of *sorbus,* the name given by the Romans to the European mountain ash (*Sorbus domestica*) that bears a somewhat similar fruit. In those regions where Elizabethan pronunciation has persisted, shadbush is still called sarvis tree.

Native range: Me. to Ga. Zone 3. There are several native species ranging from suckering shrubs to medium sized trees.

SILVERBELL

(snowdrop tree)
Halesia carolina L.
Storax family (Styracaceae)

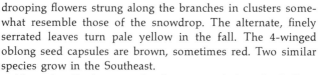

The silverbell is a small understory tree. Appearing with the
leaves in April–May, its white,
drooping flowers strung along the branches in clusters somewhat resemble those of the snowdrop. The alternate, finely
serrated leaves turn pale yellow in the fall. The 4-winged
oblong seed capsules are brown, sometimes red. Two similar
species grow in the Southeast.

Alexander Garden was the first to send the silverbell to
England in 1756. The genus name commemorates the Reverend
Stephen Hales (1677–1761) of England, a botanist and inventor
who wrote *Vegetable Staticks* . . . (1727).

Native range: Va. to Fla., Tex., Okla., and Ohio. Zone 3.

SWEET GUM

Liquidambar styraciflua L.
Witch Hazel family
(Hamamelidaceae)

Sweet gum has long been
widely cultivated as an ornamental. A large tree, with a
long, clear bole and pyramidal crown, it attains 150 feet. The
star-shaped leaves resemble those of a maple, and turn a brilliant orange red to crimson in the autumn. The long-stalked
seed capsule is a prickly ball about 1 inch in diameter, and is

coarsely spiny. Sweet gums growing from North Carolina southward produce large quantities of a fragrant, resinous sap.

Bishop Compton grew the tree from seeds sent by Banister (1681), who listed it as *Styrax folio Aceris.* In Virginia, he wrote, "it is called the sweet gumme. It weeps when wounded a white resinous gumme, of a pleasant savour, and some say very balsamick." He also sent some gum for the apothecaries to study.

The lovely genus name stems from the Latin *liquidus*, "fluid," and the Arabic *ambar*, "amber"; *styrax* is Greek for the storax tree. *Fluere*, the Latin "to flow," alludes to liquid storax, the sweet-scented sap prepared from *L. orientalis.*

Native range: Conn. to Fla., Mo., and Mex. Zone 3.

SYCAMORE

Platanus occidentalis L.
Plane Tree family (Platanaceae)

The sycamore or plane tree is a towering giant, some 170 feet tall, usually branching about 20–80 feet above the ground into a massive, spreading, open-headed tree. Its bark is light gray, greenish, or chalky white, and sloughs off in patches, giving the tree a mottled or piebald appearance. The broadly oval leaves, 3–5-lobed, usually measure up to 7 inches. The multiplex fruit is a stalked hanging sphere that gives the tree its colloquial names, "buttonwood" and "buttonball" tree.

The sycamore of the primeval forest was a colossus; huge in girth, many trees often became hollow. Chimney swifts—swallows they were called—came in many thousands to roost in these hollow trees. Early explorers recorded, too, that the sycamore's fruit was a favorite food of the now extinct Carolina parakeet. In Philadelphia, plane trees were planted about the houses and in the gardens, and seats were placed under them. Jefferson wrote from there in 1793: "I never before knew the full value of a tree. My house is embosomed in high plane trees . . . under which I breakfast, dine, write, read and receive my company."

The American plane was known in England by 1636; the oriental plane (*P. orientalis*) of southeastern Europe about 100 years earlier. Hybridizing of the American and the oriental species produced the London plane (*P. acerifolia*) so widely used in street planting today.

Platanus, the Greek name for *P. orientalis,* comes from *platys,* in allusion to the broad, flat leaves.

Native range: Me. to Fla., Tex., Nebr., and Ont. Zone 3.

TULIP TREE
Liriodendron tulipifera L.
Magnolia family
(Magnoliaceae)

This magnificent tree is said to be North America's tallest hardwood, attaining 200 feet. Tulip tree trunks rise up from the ground with almost uniform size from the ground to the first high branches. Its greenish, orange yellow banded flowers are tulip- or lily-shaped (hence the name); even its leaf form is somewhat like a conventionalized tulip design. When the winged fruits are dispersed from the cone-shaped seed clusters, the supporting cone structures persist, erect and empty. Seen in sunshine against the blue of a bright winter sky, it appears as if the tree were full of small golden flowers despite the season.

Other common names are canoewood (Daniel Boone made a canoe 60 feet long from the wood), tulip poplar, and poplar, although the tulip tree is no poplar at all. William Cobbett, the English journalist and agriculturist who spent some years in

America, wrote: "There is but one species of the tulip-tree, but that one, as the lioness said of her cub, is a tree indeed." The one other species is native to China. William Byrd observed that "everyone has some of these trees in his gardens and around the house for ornament and pleasure." Old tulip trees still exist between his house, Westover, and the James River, and there are also some on the river front of Carter's Grove. Describing Nomini Hall, his employer's plantation house, Philip Fithian wrote:

> Due East of the Great House are two Rows of tall, flourishing, beautiful, Poplars, beginning on a Line drawn from the School to the Wash-House; these Rows are something wider than the House, and are about 300 yards Long, at the Eastermost end of which is the great Road leading through Westmorland to Richmond. These Rows of Poplars form an extreemely pleasant avenue, and at the Road, through them, the House appears most romantic, at the same time that it does truly elegant.

Liriodendron is from the Greek, *leirion,* lily, and *dendron,* tree. Native range: Vt. to Fla., La., and Mich. Zone 3.

VITEX
(chaste tree)
Vitex agnus-castus L.
Verbena family
(Verbenaceae)

A shrub or small tree, vitex grows up to 20 feet. Each compound leaf is made up of 5–7 leaflets. The little light blue flowers that form spikes of blooms open in July–August.

Native to southern Europe, vitex reached England from Sicily in 1570. All parts of the plant were believed to have peculiar sedative properties. According to Pliny, the women of Athens made their pallets and beds with the leaves during the feasts of the goddess Ceres "to keep themselves chaste for the time."

Vitex probably derives from *vieo*, to plait or weave. The pliable shoots are still used by Greeks and Cretans for basket-making. *Agnus-castus* combines the Greek *hagnos* and the Latin *castus*: both words have the same meaning—chastity—and have nothing to do with the Latin *agnus*, "lamb."

Zone 5.

WALNUT, BLACK
Juglans nigra L.
Walnut family
(Juglandaceae)

Black walnut is a large tree, up to 150 feet in height, with widely spreading branches. One of man's best friends among the forest hardwoods, it is North America's finest cabinet wood and was exported to England from Jamestown as early as 1610. Almost all colonial cradles were made of black walnut, and it is the prime wood for gunstocks, absorbing more jar or recoil than any other wood. The nut is difficult to crack, and it is tedious to pick the oily sweet kernel from the nut's intricate walls. The kernel is used in confectionery and is a favorite flavoring for ice cream.

The tree was introduced into England in 1656; one at Syon Park, probably planted about 1770, now has a girth of over 16 feet and is the second largest of its kind in Britain.

Juglans is the ancient Latin name from *Jovis glaus*, "Jupiter's acorn," the name used by Pliny for the Persian walnut (*J. regia*); *nigra* means "black."

Native range: Fla. to Minn. and Tex.

Juglans regia L., the Persian walnut—commonly called English walnut—is native to southeastern Europe, the Himalayas, and

China. It is a round-headed tree, some 100 feet in height, with silver gray bark and globelike, rather thin shelled nuts.

WASHINGTON THORN

Crataegus phaenopyrum
(L.f.) Medic.
Rose family (Rosaceae)

This is reputedly one of the
most decorative of the many
American hawthorns. It was
first called the Virginia or maple-leaved hawthorn, later the Washington thorn on account of its abundance around Washington, D. C. The finely cut, 3–lobed leaves turn orange red in the fall when most other trees have lost their leaves; the bright scarlet berries persist the better part of winter. Its spikes, or thorns, 1½–2 inches, are unusually long.

Its name derives from 2 Greek words: *cratae-gus,* "strength," from the strong wood; *phaenopyrum,* "to shine," refers to the Washington thorn's shining fruit.

Native range: Pa. to Fla., Ark., and Mo. Zone 4.

THE WILLOWS

Salix
Willow family (Salicaceae)

The genus *Salix* contains over 300 species of trees and shrubs distributed chiefly in the cooler regions of the northern hemisphere. About 100 species are native to North America. The willows' chief economic value is in the toughness and suppleness of the shoots or "osiers." These have been used for centuries for wickerwork and basketmaking. Baseball bats of willow were once popular. (*S. coerulea,* the cricket bat willow, native to

[56]

England's eastern counties, provided the best cricket bats.) *Salix* is the old Latin name.

BLACK WILLOW
S. nigra Marsh.

This is the largest of the native willows, reaching 30–40 feet in height. The slender pale green leaves, finely toothed and pointed, are often scythe-shaped. In pioneering days the wood was used for making a fine charcoal for black gunpowder.

Native range: N. B. along the coast to Ga., Tex., and N. D. Zone 2.

WEEPING WILLOW
S. babylonica L.

Weeping willow is a wide-spreading tree 30–50 feet tall with long pendulous branches. It is the most notable of all weeping trees—"weeping" being a term applied to plants with drooping branches. Native to China, the tree appears in the familiar willow-tree pattern on china-ware and was introduced into England from the Euphrates River or Babylonia in 1730. Linnaeus gave it the specific name *babylonica* because he believed the tree to be native to that region. Jefferson instructed his overseer to plant these trees around the original graveyard at Monticello in 1808. The Prince Nursery catalogue of 1790 listed the weeping willow.

Zone 3.

YELLOW WOOD
Cladrastis lutea
(Michx. f.) K. Koch
Bean family (Fabaceae
[Leguminosae])

Yellow wood is a beautiful ornamental tree, growing to 50
feet. The trunk is short, the
bark silvery gray, and the frondlike foliage turns clear bright yellow in the fall. Somewhat similar to the wisteria, the fragrant ivory white blossoms with clawed petals appear in June in many flowered drooping clusters 10–20 inches long and are succeeded by short-stalked seedpods 2–4 inches in length.

André Michaux, riding in the woods near Fort Blount, Ten-
nessee, discovered the tree on the last day of February 1796. Snow lay on the ground and it was not until some days later that he returned to collect the seeds. Michaux also discovered that the inside bark of the roots provided a yellow dye. The tree was later established in Europe from seeds sent by his son François, who gathered them when he was in Nashville.

Cladrastis, "little branch" in Greek, describes the brittle twigs; *lutea*, "yellow."

Native range: Rare and local, N. C. to Ala., Mo., and the Ohio Valley. Zone 5.

YEW, ENGLISH

Taxus baccata L.
Yew family (Taxaceae)

English yew, with its short
thick trunk, is a heavily
branched evergreen tree up to
60 feet. The leaves, spirally arranged, are dark glossy green
above, pale green beneath. A poisonous, hard-shelled seed is
enclosed in the fleshy red berrylike cup. Yew, a favorite topiary
plant, is long-lived, sometimes surviving more than a thousand
years. It is a native to Europe, Britain, and parts of Asia. There
are other species in North America and eastern Asia.

Custis, writing in the spring of 1741 to Collinson, described
the severe winter just past. It caused dreadful havoc in his
garden, but the "cedars and yews and Holly stood it." A hard
frost the following winter did, however, burn the south side of
his "fine yew balls and pyramids which were established for
more than 20 years."

Taxus is the old Latin name, akin to the Greek *Taxos* of
Dioscorides used by Pliny; *baccata* means "furnished with berries."

Zone 1.

SHRUBS

ALTHEA

(Rose-of-Sharon)
Hibiscus syriacus L.
(syn. *Althaea frutex*)
Mallow family (Malvaceae)

There are more than 1,000
species of *Hibiscus* in temperate
and tropical countries around
the world, but althea is the only hardy shrub among them. It is
a much branched shrub up to 15 feet tall, with sharp-toothed
leaves that are 3–lobed or unlobed. The flowers, blooming July
to August, are typically 5–petaled, 3 inches across, bell-shaped,
and solitary in the axils of the leaves, with a color range of
white to pink, magenta, and violet blue. The fruit is a dry,
5–valved capsule.

Native to China and India, rose-of-Sharon reached England
via Syria before 1596—hence the specific name *syriacus*. *Hibiscus*
is the Greek name used by Dioscorides for a species of mallow
(see rose mallow). Althea, the more common spelling of the
genus *Althaea,* means a cure, or something that heals, and refers
to the medicinal use of some species.

Jefferson, Washington, and Lady Skipwith grew the "double
white, and common Althaea."

Native range: Zone 3.

THE AZALEAS

Rhododendron
Heath family (Ericaceae)

In earlier times, *Azalea* and *Rhodora* were listed as distinct and
separate genera; now the genus *Rhododendron* includes both. The

greatest concentration of wild species occurs in parts of China, Tibet, India, and Burma. Japan and North America have relatively few "true" rhododendrons but many lovely azaleas.

Rhododendron is from the Greek *rhodo-dendron,* "rose-tree."

FLAME AZALEA
R. calendulaceum (Michx.) Torr.

Flame azalea sometimes grows 10 feet tall. The 5–7 funnel-shaped flowers, 2 inches wide, yellow to orange scarlet, open in May just before the leaves. William Bartram called it the fiery azalea "as being expressive of the appearance of its flowers, which are in general of the colour of the finest red lead, orange and bright gold, as well as yellow and cream colour . . . the clusters of blossoms cover the shrubs in such incredible profusion on the hillsides, that suddenly opening to view from the dark shades, we are alarmed at the apprehension of the hill being set on fire." He declared it "the most gay and brilliant flowering shrub yet known." It still ranks as one of the most brilliantly colored azaleas, and figures in the parentage of many fine orange and scarlet hybrids.

Calendulaceum, "calendulalike," refers to the orange yellow color of the flower.

Native range: Pa. to Ga., Ala., and Ohio. Zone 4.

PINXTER FLOWER AZALEA
R. nudiflorum (L.) Torr.

Pinxter azalea is a much branched shrub 4–8 feet tall.

The faintly scented pink or whitish flowers, each with 5 long stamens, open on the still leafless twigs in April or May.

Dutch settlers in Pennsylvania gave it the name "pinxter" because it bloomed at the church festival of Pentecost or Whitsuntide; pingsterbloem—"Pingster bloom." The Ghent azaleas are the result of eighteenth-century hybridization in Europe between this species and the flame azalea with strains of the Asiatic *R. luteum.*

Nudiflorum is the Latin for "naked flower" because the flowers open before the leaves.

Native range: Mass. to S. C., Tenn., and Ohio. Zone 4.

THE BAYBERRIES
Myrica
Bayberry family (Myricaceae)

There are about 50 species of *Myrica,* which are aromatically fragrant evergreen or deciduous trees or shrubs native to the temperate and subtropical parts of both hemispheres. Two species are found along the coastal areas of the eastern states: wax myrtle (*M. cerifera* L.), and bayberry (*M. pensylvanica* Loisel), which ranges on the east coast from Newfoundland to North Carolina and is abundant on Virginia's Eastern Shore. Wax myrtle, called just myrtle in colonial days, is now generally known as bayberry or southern bayberry in tidewater Virginia. Both species bear blue gray berries with a waxy or resinous covering. The wax, obtained by submerging the berries in boiling water and skimming off the greenish oil as it rises and floats on the surface, is used to make bayberry candles.

WAX MYRTLE
(bayberry)
M. cerifera L.

This shrub or small tree, in some areas up to 20–30 feet

high, bears tiny blue gray berries in clusters along the twigs; both leaves and berries are fragrant. Robert Beverley wrote in his *History and Present State of Virginia* (1705):

> At the Mouth of their Rivers, all along upon the Sea and Bay, and near many of their Creeks and Swamps, grows the Myrtle, bearing a berry, of which they make a hard brittle wax, of a curious green Colour, which by refining becomes almost transparent. Of this they make Candles, which are never greasie to the Touch, nor melt with lying in the hottest Weather. Neither does the Snuff of these ever offend the Smell, like that of a Tallow candle; but, instead of being disagreeable, if an Accident puts a Candle out, it yields a pleasant Fragrancy to all that are in the Room; insomuch, that nice People often put them out, on purpose to have the Incense of the expiring Snuff.

William Byrd II said that because of the color, transparency, and fragrance of the wax, bayberry candles "sold at expensive prices." Virginia was exporting myrtle wax candles by 1752, and in 1771 Williamsburg merchants were selling candlesticks designed to hold the half-ounce green wax candles.

Myri-ca is an old Greek name, possibly for tamarisk.

Native range: N. J. to Fla., Tex., and Ark. Zone 4.

BEAUTY BERRY

(French mulberry)
Callicarpa americana L.
Verbena family
(Verbenaceae)

This shrub is 4–5 feet tall and is cultivated for its distinctive fruits. The tapered leaves are 4–6 inches long and bluntly serrate. The inconspicuous little light blue flowers open June–July, tightly bunched in the leaf angles, and are followed by the highly ornamental purple berries, which are strung along the slender arching branches at intervals in ringlike clusters and persist into early winter after the leaves have fallen.

The shrub may perhaps be called French mulberry because of some association with the French in the West Indies. "Mulberry" refers to the color mulberry, a rich purple; *Calli-carpa* is the Greek for "beauty" and "fruit."

Native range: Md. to Fla. and the West Indies, Tex., and Okla. Zone 6.

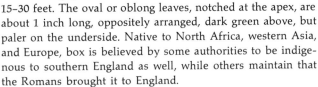

BOX, COMMON
Buxus sempervirens L.
Boxwood family (Buxaceae)

Common box is a spreading, bushy shrub, usually wider than it is high, or a small tree 15–30 feet. The oval or oblong leaves, notched at the apex, are about 1 inch long, oppositely arranged, dark green above, but paler on the underside. Native to North Africa, western Asia, and Europe, box is believed by some authorities to be indigenous to southern England as well, while others maintain that the Romans brought it to England.

The wood, close-grained, and of bonelike hardness, was used by the Greeks for making combs and musical instruments and for many other purposes. John Evelyn, in his *Silva* (1662), extolled boxwood: "The excellency of the *wood*" compensated for the "unagreeableness of its smell." He said that turners, engravers, and makers of combs, pipes, and mathematical instruments prized the wood, and that the roots of the tree, after various processes of polishing and grinding, provided the inlayer and cabinetmaker with "pieces rarely undulated, and full of variety." A crosscut section of the root has, for centuries, been unsurpassed for wood engravers. The inlay work on the staircase in the rebuilt Governor's Palace in Williamsburg is of box and holly.

For centuries regarded as a great ornamental, boxwood is a favorite plant for topiary work (the pruning and training of evergreens into various contrived shapes).

Buxus, the Latin name for box, was derived from the Greek

pukens, meaning close or dense. Boxes of boxwood were called *pyxides,* from which originated the Roman Catholic "pyx," the sacred chest containing the Host.

Zone 5.

DWARF BOX

B. sempervirens L.
"suffruticosa"

Dwarf, or edging box, a distinctive freak form perpetrated
in cultivation, grows far more
slowly and has smaller oval leaves than common box. It does
not produce seed and must be propagated by cuttings. The
plant is usually less than 3 feet high, although old plants
growing in the lush Virginia climate are 6–7 feet tall and when
left untrimmed become billowing, undulating masses.

Suffruticosa, "shrublike."

Zone 5.

CORAL BERRY

(Indian currant)
*Symphoricarpos
orbiculatus* Moench
Honeysuckle family
(Caprifoliaceae)

Coral berry is a bushy shrub,
3–7 feet in height, with slender
upright branchlets and oval
leaves up to 1½ inches long. In June or July, the tiny bell-like
white blooms are bunched close together along the stems. The
succeeding dusky red berries, no more than ¼ inch across,
almost hide the arching branches. It was generally believed that
a concoction made of the powdered root was, as Clayton said,
"an infallible remedy against intermittent malarial fever."

[65]

Some 13 species of *symphoricarpos* are native to North America; 1 other species is found in Mexico and 1 in western China.

The genus name, from the Greek "to bear together" and "fruit," alludes to the massed fruits; *orbiculatus,* "circular," refers to the shape of the fruit.

Native range: Que. to Va., Ohio, Colo., and B. C. Zone 2.

FRINGE TREE

Chionanthus virginicus L.
Olive family (Oleaceae)

In May the white fringed flowers hide the unfurling light green leaves in what appears to be an airy-fairy dusting of snow. They are followed by grape-like clusters of blue berries, and the leaves turn yellow in the fall. This large shrub or slender tree grows up to 30 feet. Jefferson, in his *Notes on the State of Virginia,* included it as an ornamental, calling it the "Fringe or snow-drop tree, *Chionanthus Virginica.*"

The genus name is from the Greek words *chion* and *anthos,* "snow" and "flower."

Native range: Sparsely from N. J. to Fla., Okla., and Tex. Zone 3.

GROUNDSEL TREE

(saltbush)
Baccharis halimifolia L.
Aster family (Asteraceae [Compositae])

This much-branched shrub, up to 12 feet high, is one of the very few woody members of the Aster (Compositae) family. The serrated leaves have yellow spots that contain resin. The inconspicuous flowers, in late summer, are followed by striking billows of white fluffy down on female plants in the fall. The shrub is conspicuous around Jamestown and along the parkways into Williamsburg.

Its flowers resemble those of the groundsel weed (*Senecio vulgaris*), hence "groundsel." *Baccharis* is the Latin name of a plant offered to Bacchus; *halimifolia*, from the Greek *halimos*, refers to the salt plant native to the Mediterranean region.

Native range: Coastal and marshlands from Mass. to Fla., Tex., and Mex. Zone 4.

THE HYDRANGEAS
Hydrangea
Saxifrage family
(Saxifragaceae)

The genus contains 80 species. Some are woody shrubs; others are root-climbers. They are found in the wild in North and South America and Asia. *Hydrangea* is from the Greek words *hydor* and *aggeion*, "water" and "vessel," describing the shape of the cuplike fruit capsule.

OAKLEAF HYDRANGEA
H. quercifolia Bartr.

Oakleaf hydrangea is a widespread, handsome shrub 4–6 feet high. It is so called because the broad, oval, and lobed leaves, 3–8 inches long, resemble those of the red oak. The flowers, white with a faint green tinge at the base of the petals, are borne in June in broad panicles up to 12 inches long. After the blooming season is over they turn rosy purple and persist into late summer. The shrub was discovered by William Bartram in Georgia in 1773.

Native range: Ga. to Fla. and
Miss. Zone 5.

WILD (or SMOOTH) HYDRANGEA

H. arborescens L.

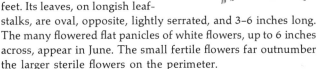

This is a low-growing shrub, attaining a height of but 3–4 feet. Its leaves, on longish leaf-stalks, are oval, opposite, lightly serrated, and 3–6 inches long. The many flowered flat panicles of white flowers, up to 6 inches across, appear in June. The small fertile flowers far outnumber the larger sterile flowers on the perimeter.

Collinson was probably the first to grow the wild hydrangea, for in a letter of 1746 he wrote, "My Hydrangea, perhaps the first in England, flowered in . . . my garden at Mill-Hill."

Unfortunately, the specific name is a poor one. *Arborescens*, which means "treelike," is not at all descriptive of this small shrub.

Native range: N. Y. to Fla., La., and Iowa. Zone 3.

LILAC, COMMON

Syringa vulgaris L.
Olive family (Oleaceae)

This well-known garden shrub blooms in April and May in fragrant clusters of "lilac" colored and white flowers. Augerius de Busbecq, ambassador from

Ferdinand I, emperor of Austria and of the Holy Roman Empire, to Suleiman the Magnificent, sultan of the Turkish Empire, brought the shrub to Europe when he returned to Vienna in 1562. By 1597 Gerard had lilacs in his garden "in very great Plenty." Lilac reached the American colonies early. In Peter Collinson's opinion, John Custis had "undoubtedly the best collection" in Virginia; lilacs do not, however, thrive in the hot and humid tidewater climate and are seen at their best farther north. Forcing the flowering sprays for out-of-season blooms was practiced in France from 1774 onward.

Syringa comes from the Greek *syrinx,* a pan-pipe. The Turks made pipes from the hollow, pithy wood.

Zone 2.

The Persian lilac (*S. persica* L.) has smaller leaves and flowers and a more pliant stem than that of the common lilac. Native to gardens in Persia and India, it was brought to Europe early. Custis, in a letter of April 1741 to Collinson, said that his "persian lilock was full of flowers."

MOCK ORANGE
Philadelphus coronarius L.
Saxifrage family
(Saxifragaceae)

Mock orange is a spreading round bush up to 12 feet tall. The creamy white, sweet-scented flowers, reminiscent of orange blossom, open in clusters of 5–7 in May–June. Native to southeastern Europe and southwestern Asia, the shrub was brought to Vienna along with the common lilac by de Busbecq in 1562.

At first lilac and mock orange were classified together and were called syringa. This led to a confusion in nomenclature that still persists, although mock orange was renamed *Philadelphus* early in the seventeenth century and was confirmed for the genus by Linnaeus. William Bartram referred to the shrub as "Philadelphus," Lady Skipwith as "Syringa or Mock Orange."

Philadelphus (literally translated from the ancient Greek it means "brotherly love") was first applied to an identified shrub perhaps to commemorate a garden loving Egyptian king, Ptolemy Philadelphus (285–246 B.C.). *Coronarius* means "garlanding," used for garlands.

Zone 2.

P. inodorus L., native to southeastern North America, is also used in Colonial Williamsburg's gardens.

MOUNTAIN LAUREL
Kalmia latifolia L.
Heath family (Ericaceae)

Mountain laurel is a round-topped evergreen shrub, usually 4–10 feet high, which occasionally becomes a small tree. The many-flowered clusters of blooms, 4–5 inches across, open in May. Each individual cup-shaped flower, white or pale rose and less than an inch across, is faintly imprinted with purple dots. Calico-bush is one of the shrub's common names, the flowers being likened to polka-dotted calico; spoon-wood is another. The Indians made spoons and trowels from the wood of the root, which is soft and easily worked when newly dug and becomes hard and smooth when dry. Kalm, for whom Linnaeus named the plant, took an Indian-made spoon of mountain laurel home with him as a souvenir of his American travels.

Mountain laurel was on occasion referred to in correspondence as ivy. This led to some confusion in interpreting what plant was intended. In writing to Custis, Collinson referred to the shrub, "by some Improperly called Ivy." In a letter to John Bartram he said: "In a few days will the glorious Mountain

Laurel, or great Chamaerhododendron appear with its charming clusters of flowers."

Latifolia is the Latin for "broad leaved." The shrub belongs, as do the broad-leaved rhododendrons, to the Heath family—hence Chamaerhododendron.

Native range: N. E. to Fla. and La. Zone 3.

POMEGRANATE

Punica granatum L.
Pomegranate family
(Punicaceae)

The pomegranate, a shrub that grows up to 20 feet, has shining, lance-shaped leaves, and vermilion carnationlike flowers in June–July. The fruit, the size of an orange, has a hard leathery rind and, when ripe, turns red and splits open, revealing the numerous crimson seeds within. The double-flowered forms make a spectacular show.

Byrd said that pomegranates were found "at the homes of the fanciers and became exceptionally beautiful and good in Virginia." Catesby saw them growing in great perfection in Byrd's own garden. On September 20, 1711, Byrd sent 4 pomegranates from Westover to the governor in Williamsburg.

Native to the eastern Mediterranean and eastward to northwestern India, pomegranate is one of the oldest fruits in cultivation; it is mentioned in the Bible and the Odyssey. *Punica* is the old Latin name for Carthage. Gerard concluded that *granatum* alluded to the numbers of pomegranates planted by the Moors in Granada, Spain. The fruit appears on that city's arms, is worked into the stone patterns of old garden walks, and is regarded as Granada's symbol.

Zone 5.

ROSE, CHEROKEE

Rosa laevigata Michx.
Rose family (Rosaceae)

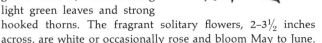

This rose is a rampant evergreen climber, with shining
light green leaves and strong
hooked thorns. The fragrant solitary flowers, 2–3½ inches
across, are white or occasionally rose and bloom May to June.

This rose, native to China, was brought to England in 1759
and was known as *R. sinica*. Later, when introduced into the
southern states, it was called the Cherokee rose, perhaps because it became naturalized there so quickly. It is now Georgia's
state flower. It was Georgia's Governor Milledge who sent the
seeds to Jefferson, who recorded in his diary on April 29, 1804,
that he had planted them in his nursery garden.

Rosa is the old Latin name for rose; *Cherokee* for one of the
great Indian tribes of the South; *laevigata* from *laevigatus,*
"smooth."

Native range: Zone 6.

Why is the Cherokee the only rose included in this handbook? Obviously, it is of special interest to rose lovers in the
southern states and is a carefree grower. In general, the culture
of old roses is impracticable here, partly because of the climate
and partly for reasons of maintenance. But a few other roses
native to the eastern states are to be seen in the gardens of
Colonial Williamsburg, including the swamp rose (*R. palustris*).

STEWARTIA, MOUNTAIN
Stewartia ovata (Cav.) Weath.
Tea family (Theaceae)

The mountain stewartia is a lovely and rare native shrub or small tree growing up to 15 feet in height. The solitary white flowers, in June, are 2–3 inches across; the scallop-margined petals surround a boss of numerous white or purple filaments and orange anthers. Related to the camellias, the shrub is sometimes called "mountain camellia." However, the Reverend John Clayton (distantly related to Clayton the botanist), rector of James City Parish (1684–1686), thought the flower was like "the false flour of the dogg tree" (dogwood). Some long-time natives of the counties around Williamsburg still call it summer dogwood when they find it in the woods.

There are two native stewartias. Early botanists confused the one with the other; there was also confusion with the specific name. *S. ovata*, probably the first of the two plants described, was known as *S. malachodendron*; this specific name is now properly applied to the Virginia stewartia or "silky camellia."

Mitchell sent the stewartia to England in 1741. Catesby included it in his *Natural History*, drawing the plant from one sent him the following year by Clayton, the botanist. Catesby wrote: "For this elegant Plant I am obliged to my good friend Mr. Clayton, who sent it me from *Virginia*, and three months after its arrival it blossomed in my garden at Fulham, in May 1742." Linnaeus upheld the name Catesby gave the genus in honor of John Stuart (1713–1792), earl of Bute, who was an enthusiastic naturalist and a keen botanist.

Ovata, meaning egg-shaped, refers to the small oval seed capsules.

Native range: Va. and Ky. south to Ga. and Ala.

STRAWBERRY BUSH

(burning bush, heart's-a-bustin')
Euonymus americanus L.
Bittersweet family (Celastraceae)

This shrub, up to 8 feet high,
is conspicuous for its green
stems, but it has inconspicuous
flowers. The fruits make the show. The 3–5-lobed strawberry
colored capsules, $\frac{1}{2}$ inch across, burst open in early fall and
reveal the orange colored seeds within. The shrub is grown as
an ornamental in Colonial Williamsburg and is common in the
woods nearby.

　　Euonymus is the ancient Greek name for the European species.
Native range: N. Y. to Fla., Tex., and Okla. Zone 4.

THE SUMACS

Rhus
Cashew family (Anacardiaceae)

The trees and shrubs known as sumacs are very diverse in
appearance and are found in both hemispheres. Some are
known for their brilliant autumn color, others for their use in
dyeing, tanning, and the production of lacquer, varnish, and
wax. Certain species have a poisonous oil, toxicodendrol, se-
creted on their leaves; persons coming into contact with the
plant sometimes suffer a painful, itching skin eruption.

　　Sumach was the Persian name; *Rhus* from the Greek for "red,"
was used by Theophrastus.

FRAGRANT SUMAC
Rhus aromatica Ait.

The greenish yellow flower clusters of this low sprawling shrub, 2–6 feet high, open March–April before the leaves. The three leaflets, 2–3 inches long, are coarsely toothed and aromatic. Although they closely resemble the leaves of poison ivy, they contain no poisonous oil. The fruits are red and hairy; those of the native poison sumac (*Rhus vernix* L.) are white. Fragrant sumac was planted as an ornamental in colonial gardens.

Native range: Ont. to Minn. and south to Fla. and La. Zone 3.

STAGHORN SUMAC
R. typhina L.

Staghorn sumac, a shrub or tree that grows up to 30 feet, was introduced into England before 1629. It was known as "the Bucks horne tree of Virginia," the reddish brown velvety branchlets being likened to the antlers of a stag when "in the velvet." The greenish flowers, in panicles 4–8 inches long, open in June and July. With its hairy, crimson seed clusters and its leaves in mottled shades of orange, purple, and vermilion, staghorn sumac makes a brilliant show in the fall. Banister said that the pulp and skin of the berries were used in Virginia to make vinegar and to season meats, the roots were used to reduce fever, and the gum was a remedy for toothache. Leaves and twigs were also used in dyeing and tanning.

Typhina alludes to its supposed medical virtues in the treatment of typhoid fever.

Native range: Que. to Fla., Tex., and Kans. Zone 3.

Two other native sumacs are shining sumac (*R. copallina*) and smooth sumac (*R. glabra*). Both are shrubs or small trees with greenish flowers in dense panicles in July and August. The succeeding fruits of shining sumac are crimson and hairy; those of the smooth sumac are scarlet with a sticky covering or down.

SWEET SHRUB
(Carolina allspice)
Calycanthus floridus L.
Calycanthus family
(Calycanthaceae)

Sweet shrub grows up to 10 feet and has stiff maroon colored flowers, the petals enclosing a tuft of short yellow stamens. Leaves, wood, bark, and flowers are all spicily and fruitily fragrant. Children once nibbled the stems and leaves and carried blooms in their handkerchiefs on the way to school, later to pinch the flower cluster and sniff it during lessons.

Catesby, the first to mention the shrub, found it about 100 miles deep in the backcountry of South Carolina. He was responsible for its introduction—or perhaps its reintroduction—into England, and for its being cultivated in Charleston gardens in the eighteenth century.

The genus name is from the Greek *calyx* and *anthos,* meaning "cup" and "flower."

Native range: Va. and W. Va. to Fla. and Miss. Zone 4.

TATARIAN HONEYSUCKLE

Lonicera tatarica L.
Honeysuckle family
(Caprifoliaceae)

This is a bushy shrub growing
up to 10 feet. The pink, crimson, or white flowers, usually
in pairs, appear in May and June, and are succeeded by bright
red opalescent berries.

It is native in Russia and Turkestan; in 1752 Philip Miller
raised plants from seed sent to him from the imperial garden at
St. Petersburg "to which they were conveyed from Tartary."

Lonicera commemorates the German naturalist-physician
Adam Lonicer (1528–1586). "Tatarian" for the country of the
Tatars; "honeysuckle" takes its name from *hunisuce,* the
Anglo-Saxon for privet.

Zone 2.

THE VIBURNUMS

Viburnum
Honeysuckle family
(Caprifoliaceae)

The large *Viburnum* genus is spread over Europe, North America, China, and Japan. Only the European and American species
were known in the eighteenth century. The genus name is the
Latin for the wayfaring tree, *V. lantana* L., native to Europe and
Britain.

SNOWBALL

(Guelder-rose)
Viburnum opulus L. "sterile"

Snowball, the garden form of
V. opulus, the European cran-
berry bush, gets its name from
the white snowball-like 3–5-inch-thick bosses in May–June. Its
opposite leaves resemble those of the maple.

Its name, "Snow-ball tree," appeared in Miller's *Gardener's
Dictionary* of 1759. Guelder-rose is after Gelderland, a province
of the Netherlands; the name was formerly given to *V. opulus,*
which was abundant in Gelderland, where the snowball viburnum probably originated. *Populus,* "poplar," gives no clue to the
origin of *opulus,* which is derived from it. "Sterile" because it is
fruitless.

Native range: Zone 2.

BLACK HAW

V. prunifolium L.

This bushy tree, up to 30 feet
tall, has dark green foliage and
flattish clusters of creamy
flowers. It is at its best in autumn, its blue black berries con-
trasting with the deep burgundy red foliage.

Collinson, writing to Bartram in 1739, thanked him heartily
for the black haws: "I wish I had a plant that bears Fruit of this
Tree, the Berries are a pretty Fruite to Eat by some are call'd
Indian Sweetmeat being as I am told a Usuall present from the
Indians to their Guests."

Native range: Conn. to Fla., Tex., and Kans. Zone 3.

[78]

HIGHBUSH CRANBERRY
V. trilobum Marsh.
(syn. *V. americanum* auch.)

This native species, a shrub
growing to 25 feet, is so similar
to the European Guelder-rose
V. opulus that some botanists classify it as a geographical form.
The leaves are 3–lobed (*trilobum*), 2–5 inches, and longer than
the European species; the flat inflorescence has white marginal
flowers that are showy and sterile. The berries, in September–
October, are bright scarlet.

Native range: Nfld. to B. C., south to Pa., Iowa, Wyo., and
Wash. Zone 6 northward.

LAURUSTINUS
V. tinus L.

Laurustinus, an evergreen
shrub that grows 10–15 feet, is
native to the Mediterranean
region and was brought to England in 1560. The leaves are a
dark lustrous green, and the white flowers open in clusters 2–4
inches across from pink buds in February–March.

Batty Langley, the English author of architectural and gardening texts, suggested in 1728 that a "small Hedge of Laurus-
Tinus Plants, planted in large Flower Pots" was the best ornament for little used rooms in wintertime.

Tinus was a pre-Linnaean name for the plant.

Zone 6.

WITCH HAZEL

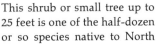

Hamamelis virginiana L.
Witch Hazel family
(Hamamelidaceae)

This shrub or small tree up to
25 feet is one of the half-dozen
or so species native to North
America and eastern Asia. It was the first of its genus to reach
England and is the name-plant of the Witch Hazel family. Witch
hazel was growing in Collinson's garden by 1736. Clayton sent
Catesby another plant in a case of earth in 1743—"It arrived in
Christmas, and was then in full blossom." The small, faintly
fragrant, yellow flowers, with their narrow twisted petals and
brownish calyx, did not appeal to Catesby. They made "no
show," and he concluded that Nature designed the shrub "for
the stricter eyes of the botanist." And it is, in fact, a botanical
curiosity. The flowers appear as the leaves fall in autumn, and
the seed pods of the previous year split open explosively and
jettison their two black seeds as far as 25 feet.

The Indians used the inner bark, applying it externally for
sore eyes and inflammations. Today, the partially dried leaves
are distilled to provide a lotion containing water and alcohol
that is used primarily as a household remedy.

Among the various versions of the origin of the name "witch
hazel" is that American settlers used the twigs for water
divining like those of the European hazel were used in England.
This is commonly called "witching a well."

Hamamelis comes from the Greek *hama,* "together," and *mela,*
"fruit," in reference to the flowers and fruit being on the tree at
the same time (the fruit takes a year to ripen).

Native range: N. S. to Ga. and Nebr. Zone 2.

WOODY VINES

CAROLINA JESSAMINE

(yellow jessamine)
Gelsemium sempervirens (L.)
Jaume Saint-Hilaire
Logania family (Loganiaceae)

This evergreen vine sometimes
reaches 20 feet. In April and
May the delicately fragrant
5–lobed trumpet-shaped yellow flowers open either singly or in
bunches of 2–6 and provide a mass of bloom.

The vine was introduced into England about 1640 and was
once called the Virginia jasmine, whose high climbing stalks
"form at a distance a grand figure for the sway they bear."

The genus name is the Latinized form of *gelsemino,* the Italian
name for the true jasmine.

Native range: Ark. Zone 6.

CROSS VINE

(trumpet flower)
Anisostichus capreolata (L.)
Bureau (syn. *Bignonia
capreolata* L.)
Bignonia family (Bignoniaceae)

Cross vine is an evergreen
climber, so-named for the +
seen in a cross section of the
stem. The orange reddish trumpetlike flowers, usually blotched
inside with magenta, appear April–May, 2–5 blooms bunched
together on the stem. Cross vine somewhat resembles the

trumpet vine *Campsis radicans,* which blooms from July to September. Catesby illustrated cross vine in his *Natural History.*

Bignonia commemorates Louis XIV's librarian, Abbé Bignon (1662–1743). *Capreolata* suggests that the plant has tendrils.

Native range: Md. to Fla., La., Mo., and Ill. Zone 4.

GRAPE VINES
Vitis
Grape family (Vitaceae)

Liberty Hyde Bailey, in describing the development of the American grape in his *Sketch of the Evolution of Native Fruits,* wrote: "North America is a natural vineland . . . the first record of America is of its grapes." He referred to Leif, son of Eric, the old Norse navigator. Leif, also a navigator, touched the northeastern shores about the year 1000. One of the exploring parties that he sent out found vines hung with their fruit, so Leif called the country Vinland.

Amadas and Barlow, the English sea captains sent out by Sir Walter Raleigh to reconnoiter the North Carolina coastline in 1584, found the land "so full of grapes as the very beating and surge of the sea overflowed them, of which we found such plenty, as well there as in all places else, both on the sand and on the green hills as in the plains, as well on every little shrub, as also climbing towards the tops of high cedars."

Captain John Smith saw in and around Jamestown (1607–1609) a great abundance of vines that in some places "climbe the toppes of the highest trees." And Robert Beverley, in his *History and Present State of Virginia* (1705), wrote of grape vines growing wild in an "incredible Plenty and Variety."

"Grape" is a translation of the old German *chrapho,* "hook," and thus alludes to the vine's clinging tendrils. The Latin name, *vitis,* identifies *V. vinifera* L., the wine grape of the Bible.

FOX GRAPE

V. labrusca L.

The fox grape is a strong, high climber. It bears a few large purple black grapes, which have a strong musky or "foxy" flavor, to the cluster. Beverley used the name "fox grape" for this species because of the rank taste, which is like the smell of a fox. He added that it made admirable tarts. In the early days, however, the term fox grape was applied to various kinds of native grapes, although it is now restricted to *V. labrusca.*

Beauchamp Plantagenet, in his account of New Albion (a part of present-day Delaware), used the verb "to fox" for intoxicate. He said that a second draught of wine made from the muscat grape "will fox a reasonable pate for moneths old." Like other settlers, Plantagenet applied muscat and other foreign names to the wild vines that bore a resemblance to named European varieties. Virginia plantation owners preferred imported European wines to the local product, although William Byrd II, when running the Dividing Line between Virginia and North Carolina, said that he drank tolerably good wine pressed from the wild grape. Wine made from native vines was not much enjoyed until their hybridization in the nineteenth century.

The fox grape is quite variable in the wild and is the source of many hybrids. The Concord grape developed from a chance seedling in a Massachusetts garden that is believed to have sprung from a wild fox grape growing nearby. The vine is sometimes grown as an ornamental for its abundant and attractive foliage.

Native range: Me. to Ga., Ala., and Mich. Zone 3.

MUSCADINE GRAPE
V. rotundifolia Michx.

This is the vine that so amazed
Barlow and Amadas. It is a long
climbing, hard-wooded vine,
with fruit borne singly or 3–5 grapes to a bunch. The fruit is
dull purple, tough skinned, and has a musky taste.

Rotundifolia means "round-leaved."

Native range: W. Va. and Del. to Fla., Tex., and Mo. Zone 5.

A bronze colored muscadine, the scuppernong was originally
found on Roanoke Island, North Carolina, by Sir Walter Raleigh's first colonists there. The grapes are yellowish, sweet, and
fragrant, growing 4–6 in a cluster. Many varieties of the muscadine have since been selected and propagated, some of which
bear purple grapes, while others are bronze like the scuppernong. Scuppernong wine is a wine of the South.

HONEYSUCKLE, CORAL
(trumpet honeysuckle)
Lonicera sempervirens L.
Honeysuckle family
(Caprifoliaceae)

Coral honeysuckle is a climbing vine that is evergreen in its
southern range. The flowers
are gaudy but scentless. The 2–inch-long corollas are orange
red on the outside and yellow within. This honeysuckle is at the

height of its bloom in April and May, but a few blooms may be found in the summer months.

The vine caught the eye of discerning colonial gardeners, including William Byrd II. Beverley wrote of a summerhouse at Westover "set round with the *Indian* Honey-Suckle, which all the Summer is continually full of sweet Flowers, in which these Birds [humming birds] delight exceedingly."

Lonicera commemorates the German naturalist-physician Adam Lonicer (1528–1586). Honeysuckle takes its name from *hunisuce,* the Anglo-Saxon for privet.

Native range: Mass. to Fla., Tex., and Nebr. Zone 3.

The heavily fragrant Japanese honeysuckle (*L. japonica*), so familiar along roadsides and festooning fences and trees along the eastern seaboard, has become an invasive and pestilential weed.

IVY, COMMON
(English ivy)
Hedera helix L.
Ginseng family (Araliaceae)

This evergreen climbs up to 100 feet and has triangular, 3–5-lobed, dark green veined leaves. In October it bears umbels of yellowish green flowers that are followed by dull inky black berries. Common ivy has "sported" into numerous forms.

Native to Europe and Britain, the ivy reached the American colonies early, and former uses of the word "ivy" for mountain laurel and other plants have confused many early references (see mountain laurel).

The origin of "ivy" is obscure. *Hedera* is "cord" in the old Latin; *helix,* "spiral" in Greek, describes ivy's characteristic climbing habit.

Zone 4.

TRUMPET VINE

Campsis radicans (L.)
Seemann
Bignonia family
(Bignoniaceae)

This woody vine is a rampant
climber up to 30 feet. Each
compound leaf has 7–11 leaf-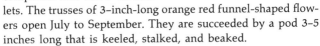
lets. The trusses of 3–inch-long orange red funnel-shaped flow-
ers open July to September. They are succeeded by a pod 3–5
inches long that is keeled, stalked, and beaked.

In his *Natural History* Catesby shows a hummingbird in flight
beside a flowering spray. He observed that hummingbirds
delighted to feed on the flowers, occasionally thrusting themselves so far into the flower that they were caught within it.

Campsis is from *kampe,* bending, referring to the curved stamens; *radicans* means "rooting," a reference to the vine's habit
of clinging by means of its aerial roots.

Native range: Pa. to Fla. and Tex. Zone 3.

VIRGINIA CREEPER

Parthenocissus quinquefolia (L.)
Planchon
Grape family (Vitaceae)

Virginia creeper reached England about 1629 and was first
known as the Virginia vine.
This strong rampant vine has alternate leaves divided into 5
leaflets and arranged finger fashion. They are pointed and
toothed along the margin, dull green above, but much lighter on

the underside, and turn bright red in the fall. Climbing to 20–40 feet, the vine clings to walls and trees by tendrils that end in adhesive disks.

Parthenocissus is Greek for "virgin ivy"; *quinquefolia* means "five-leaved."

Native range: Me. and Que. to Minn., south to Fla., Tex., and into Mex. Zone 2.

POISON IVY
R. radicans L.

Many people confuse the leaves of poison ivy and poison oak with those of Virginia creeper. Each leaf of poison ivy, *Toxicodendron radicans* (L.) Kuntze (syn. *Rhus radicans* L.), and poison oak, *Toxicodendron toxicarium* (Salisb.) Gillis (syn. *Rhus toxicodendron* L.), is composed of 3 separate leaflets. In contrast, the leaves of Virginia creeper are composed of 5 separate leaflets.

Poison ivy and poison oak are very closely related, and some botanists have not considered them to be separate species. However, they are recognized as separate species in the most recent comprehensive study of the group (Gillis, 1971).

Poison oak is a shrub, but poison ivy may occur as a shrub, as a high clinging vine, or sometimes even as a small tree.

Poison ivy occurs in both the eastern and western parts of this country, but *Toxicodendron toxicarium* is known no farther west than central Texas. Another closely related species of poison oak, *Toxicodendron diversiloba* (Torrey and Gray) Greene, occurs on the West Coast.

VIRGIN'S BOWER
(Virginia clematis)
Clematis virginiana L.
Buttercup family
(Ranunculaceae)

This native semi-evergreen clematis is a strong climber and from midsummer to fall

[87]

covers bushes and fences with an abundance of small white flowers. Three leaflets make up each serrate opposite leaf. In character with most clematis, the seeds are entwined with delicate gray curly threads.

Dioscorides gave the name *clematis* to a finely branched vine. Native range: Que. to Ga., La., Kans., and Man. Zone 4.

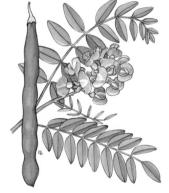

WISTERIA, AMERICAN
Wisteria frutescens (L.) Poir.
Bean family (Fabaceae
[Leguminosae])

American wisteria, one of a handful of species of woody vines found in eastern North America and eastern Asia, reaches 30–40 feet. The flowers, lilac purple in dense racemes 3–4 inches long, appear first in May, after the leaves, and continue to bloom less abundantly throughout the summer. The flowers of the more commonly cultivated Asiatic species appear before the leaves.

Catesby sent this wisteria to England in 1724 as the "Carolina Kidney Bean"—the seed pods are 2–4 inches long. Wisteria was named for Dr. Caspar Wistar (1761–1818) of Philadelphia by Nuttall, who deliberately spelled the name with an *e*. The alternatively spelled "wistaria," with an *a*, is a later adaptation.

Native range: Md. to Fla., Tex., and Ark. Zone 4.

ANNUALS, PERENNIALS, BULBS

THE ASTERS

Aster

Aster family (Asteraceae [Compositae])

There are about 600 species of asters, the majority of which are leafy stemmed perennials. Asters are most numerous in North America, although several are native to Europe. *Aster*, the Greek for "star," was first known as starwort. Michaelmas daisy, another name still common in England, came into use after 1752, when Pope Gregory's calendar revision caused Michaelmas Day (September 29) to fall 11 days earlier. This coincided with the flowering time of many of the newly introduced North American species.

NEW YORK ASTER

A. novi-belgii L.

This slender stemmed perennial, 1–3 feet, has many bright, blue violet, rayed flowers in September and October.

The seed of this aster was collected in the Dutch province of New Netherland and was sent to a German botanist in Holland who named one of the resulting seedlings *novi belgii*, the nearest Latin equivalent to New Netherland. When Charles II of England ordered the annexation of the province in 1664, New Netherland was renamed New York for the king's brother, the Duke of York. From then on the aster became known as the New York aster, although its improvised Latin name, *novi-belgii,* remained unchanged.

Native range: Nfld. to Ga.

NEW ENGLAND ASTER

A. novae-angliae L.

A stout stemmed perennial, 3–5 feet, it bears violet purple rayed flower heads 1–2½ inches across.

Novae-angliae, from New England, so named by Captain John Smith in 1614.

Native range: Que. to N. C. and Colo.

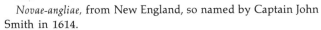

ATAMASCO LILY

(zephyr lily, Jamestown lily)
Zephyranthes atamasco (L.) Herb.
Amaryllis family
(Amaryllidaceae)

The leaves and flowers of this spring blooming bulb appear together in April and May. The narrow strap-shaped leaves are 16 inches long; the solitary flowers, 2½–4 inches, are white, flushing pink as they age.

Native to America, the species was introduced into Europe from the west, reaching England before 1629. Catesby, who illustrated it in his *Natural History,* wrote: "It is a native of

Virginia and Carolina, where in particular places the pastures are as thick sprinkled with them and Martagons, as Cowslips and Orchises are with us in England." One stretch of pastureland on Jamestown Island is still "thick" with the flower, known locally as the Jamestown lily.

Atamasco is the Indian name. Zephyr lily, *Zephyranthes*, is from the Greek *zephyros*, west wind, and *anthos*, flower.

Native range: Va. to Fla. and Miss.

THE BELLFLOWERS

Campanula
Bellflower family (Campanulaceae)

Bellflowers, from *Campanula*, "little bell," are so called on account of their bell-shaped flowers. Some 250 species, chiefly perennial, are found in the northern hemisphere, most of them in Europe.

CANTERBURY BELL

C. medium L.

This bellflower has blue, white, and pinkish flowers borne on erect stems, 2–4 feet, in May–June. It was introduced into England from southern Europe in 1597, advertised in a Boston newspaper in 1760, and listed by Lady Skipwith.

The name "Canterbury" was probably first given to the nettle-leaved bellflower *C. trachelium*, which is native to Europe and Britain. Its bell-shaped flowers dangling down in spikelike racemes resembled the small horse bells used by pilgrims to Canterbury. It is not known when the name was transferred to *C. medium*.

CHIMNEY BELLFLOWER
C. pyramidalis L.

This 4–5-foot, erect perennial was cultivated in England before 1596 for its long densely blossomed panicles of blue flowers. It was known as steeple-bells until the fashion of growing it in pots to embellish the fireplace during the summer months, a practice that still persists in England, took hold. Louis Liger in *The Retir'd Gardner* (1706) suggested that it be placed—along with tuberose, sweet basil, and other potted plants—"upon the half space before a chimney."

Pyramidalis means "pyramid-shaped."

PEACH-LEAVED BELLFLOWER
C. persicifolia L.

This bellflower, native to Britain and Europe, was also in cultivation in England before 1596 in both blue and white varieties. The double forms appeared in the eighteenth century and superseded the single kinds. It is a variable plant in cultivation. The large cup-shaped blue flowers are borne on 2–3-foot stems; the lower leaves resemble those of the peach. Today there are many named varieties of double and semi-double forms.

THE BERGAMOTS
Monarda
Mint family (Lamiaceae [Labiatae])

Native to North America, the bergamots or monards are erect, aromatic, annual and perennial plants belonging to the mint family. Like the mints, they have square stems and opposite leaves. Named for the Spanish botanist-physician, Dr. Nicholas Monardes, another common name for the genus is horse-mint. "Horse-mint" may best be explained by a reference in one of Banister's letters to what was probably the dotted monard (*M. punctata*): "In our way home the rich low grounds abounds with a kind of wild Balm, which being trampled by our horses as we rode thro it mightly refresh-ed us with its fragrant scent."

BEE-BALM
(scarlet bergamot)
M. didyma L.

Bee-balm is a perennial that grows up to 2–3 feet with com-pact crownlike whorls of leaflike bracts. Hummingbirds and bees throng to the wide-mouthed scarlet flowers. When in Philadelphia, Kalm observed some hummingbirds vying for "the Monards with crimson flowers." The plant, recorded in England by 1656, was presum-ably lost to cultivation until John Bartram found it at Oswego on Lake Ontario in 1744. He sent some of the seeds that he collected to Collinson, and bergamot flowered in Collinson's garden the following year. Wrote John Hill in 1757: "The modern Gardener is very well acquainted with the Plant, whose Fragrance and Colour demand a Place for it in every Collection and have made it nearly universal." A year or so later it was to be had in "plenty in Covent Garden Market."

In and around Oswego the Indians and the colonists made an infusion of the leaves, hence another common name, Oswego tea. In August 1807 Professor Benjamin Smith Barton of Phila-delphia found the Indian women in the village of Oneida "engaged in carefully collecting and preserving the flowers in baskets. They use them in the shape of a tea, and call the plant

O-jee-che—the fiery or flaming plant." According to one writer, many persons in early nineteenth-century England preferred Oswego to the tea of China.

All parts of the plant—creeping rootlets, red tinged green leaves, sturdy square stems—are strongly aromatic. It was named "bergamot" because its fragrance was like that of the bergamot orange, an orange-lemon hybrid (named after the town of Bergamo in northern Italy) rich in an aromatic oil that was used in perfumery as early as 1688.

Didyma, meaning "paired," alludes to the 2 protruding stamens.

Native range: Que. to Mich. and south to Ga.

WILD BERGAMOT

M. fistulosa L.

Wild bergamot is taller than but very similar to bee-balm, with lilac blue flowers that bloom from late summer into autumn. John Tradescant the Younger took the plant home with him from Virginia in 1637.

Fistulosa, "hollow" or "reedlike," refers to the stem.

Native range: Me. to Ga. and Tex., west to Sask. and B. C.

BOUNCING BET

Saponaria officinalis L.
Pink family (Caryophyllaceae)

Bouncing Bet is a perennial 1–3 feet tall with dense clusters of pink and white flowers in July.
The *flora-plena* variety, which has double white flowers, is usually seen in gardens.

The folk name suits a plant so readily adaptable. Bouncing

Bet, native to Europe and temperate Asia, naturalized rapidly in Britain after its arrival in 1629 and, on crossing the Atlantic, quickly took a firm foothold, as a garden escape, on American soil. Soapwort is another common name; mixed with water, the leaves and stems form a soaplike lather that was used as a substitute for soap and to scour wooden and pewter vessels.

Saponaria, from *sapo*, "soap."

CALENDULA
(pot marigold)
Calendula officinalis L.
Aster family (Asteraceae [Compositae])

Calendula is the marigold of English literature and is still known in England by that name. Cooks flavored their stews and soups with it and called it pot marigold. Charles Lamb, the English essayist, detested "marigolds floating in the pot." Dutch grocers kept the dried petals by the barrelful, while apothecaries used the whole plant to make a soothing ointment for skin wounds and ulcers and, as a substitute for saffron, in treating smallpox and measles.

Today's calendula, with its 2-inch orange and yellow flowers and correspondingly larger leaves, is vastly "improved" from the plant colonial gardeners knew. Brought to England from Europe about 1573, by the 1600s gardeners in Virginia and New Netherlands were growing "marigolds."

CANDYTUFT

Iberis sempervirens L.
Mustard family (Brassicaceae
[Cruciferae])

Candytuft, a common perennial, is an evergreen sub-shrub
of spreading habit that forms a
leafy mat 9–12 inches high. Flattopped clusters of snow white
flowers open in March and April; each small 4–petaled flower
stands opposite another in a square cross that is characteristic
of the family formerly called Cruciferae, "cross-bearing."

"Candytuft" and *Iberis* represent the ancient names of Crete
(Candia) and Spain (Iberia), the places of origin of many species
native to the Mediterranean region. The plant reached England
from southern Europe in 1739.

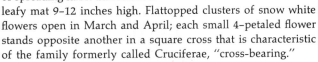

CHINA ASTER

Callistephus chinensis Nees
Aster family (Asteraceae
[Compositae])

China aster is an erect,
branching annual, with deep,
irregularly toothed leaves, that
grows to 2½ feet. The showy, daisylike solitary flower heads,
1–5 inches across, appear in almost every color except yellow,
although blue or violet predominate.

As the common name implies, it is native to China. Seeds
reached Paris in 1728 and were sent from there to Miller in
London three years later. Collinson sent seeds to Custis in 1731
and again in 1742.

From the start, China aster was extolled as a glorious autumn flower. By mid-century, James Justice, a Scottish gardener, was raising many varieties in a color range that included pink, deep carnation, blue, white, and purple. Justice recommended China asters be grown as pot-plants "to adorn Courtyards and Parlours, where they will make a most handsome Appearance." In 1770 Sir Horace Walpole described a 14-acre Paris garden in which "every walk is buttoned on each side by lines of flower-pots, which succeed in their seasons"—in all, 9,000 pots of China asters were used.

Callis-tephus from the Greek for "beautiful crown."

COCKSCOMB, COMMON
(celosia)
Celosia cristata L.
Amaranth family
(Amaranthaceae)

Cockscombs are tender annuals, their miniscule blooms compacted into many fantastic forms and often brilliantly colored. They bloom from July to October. Common cockscomb is representative of the heavy headed, crested type with widely fasciated plumes. The plant is about 9 inches high. Its dark red inflorescence, compressed and flattened, is like a cock's comb. *C. argenta* has long, dense silvery white spikes, while *C. pyramidalis* bears feathery plumes of various colors in a wider range than the crested type.

Cockscomb reached England from Asia about 1570. In 1709 Lawson described "Prince's feather [*C. pyramidalis*] very large and beautiful" in the gardens of the Carolinas; Beverley sought the seeds of what he called "Amar. Coxcomb," and Jefferson grew "cockscomb, a flower like the Prince's feather."

Celosia is from the Greek word *kelos*, meaning "burned," which describes the color and character of the inflorescence.

THE CONEFLOWERS

Rudbeckia

Aster family (Asteraceae [Compositae])

There are about 30 species of coneflowers, all native to North America. The genus was named for Olof Rudbeck (1630–1702), professor of botany at Uppsala, Sweden, and founder of the botanical garden there.

CONEFLOWERS

R. laciniata L.

Coneflower is a coarse, much branched, summer flowering perennial that grows to 12 feet. The flowers are solitary and few; their yellow rays, 1 inch or more long, droop away from the greenish thimble-shaped disk. The plant reached France in the early 1600s from the French colony in Canada, and, according to Parkinson, was "noursed up" by Vespasian Robin, herbalist at Paris to Henry IV. Robin "gave Mr. Tradescant some that has increased well with him, and thereof hath imparted to me also."

"Cone" from the prominent, thimblelike shape of the flower center; *laciniata* describing the deeply cut leaves.

Native range: Que. to Fla., La., Tex., and Ariz.

BLACK-EYED SUSAN

R. hirta L.

This familiar wildflower is a biennial or short-lived perennial. Solitary flower heads on bristly hairy stems, 1–3 feet, usually have up to 14 golden yellow rays 1–2 inches long; the disk, nearly black, turns brown as the flower head matures.

The name of the dark-centered flower may perhaps have been taken from a popular English song written in 1720:

> All in the Downs the fleet was moored,
>> The streamers waving in the wind,
> When black-eyed Susan came on board—
>> Oh, where shall I my true love find
> Tell me, ye jovial sailors, tell me true
> If my sweet William sails among your crew?

Hirta, or "hairy," refers to the hairy stems.
Native range: Mass. to Ga. and Ala.

COLUMBINE, CANADA
Aquilegia canadensis L.
Buttercup family
(Ranunculaceae)

Columbines are hardy perennials of the Northern Hemisphere.
This native columbine reached England by 1640. Like all columbines, its leaves resemble those of the buttercup. The drooping flowers, each with 5 talonlike backward pointing spurs, are brick red lined with yellow. J. Pitton de Tournefort, the great French botanist, described the flowers of the European columbine as being "composed of plain Petals intermixed with others that are hollow and horned, so that they imitate a Pidgeon with expanded Wings."

The origin of both the common and the Latin names is a matter of guesswork. Columbine from *columba,* "dove." *Aquilegia* from *aquila,* "eagle," may refer to the talonlike spurs.

Native range: East of the Rocky Mts., from Can. to the Gulf.

COREOPSIS

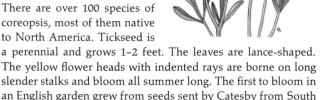

(tickseed)
Coreopsis lanceolata L.
Aster family
(Asteraceae [Compositae])

There are over 100 species of
coreopsis, most of them native
to North America. Tickseed is
a perennial and grows 1–2 feet. The leaves are lance-shaped.
The yellow flower heads with indented rays are borne on long
slender stalks and bloom all summer long. The first to bloom in
an English garden grew from seeds sent by Catesby from South
Carolina in 1724.

Coreopsis, from the Greek *koris*, a bug, and *opsis*, "like,"
alludes to the seeds being like a bug in shape and color.
Tickseed, the American name, supposedly immortalized the
tick. The specific name describes the lancelike leaves.

Native range: Ont. to Fla. and N. Mex.

CORNFLOWER

Centaurea cyanus L.
Aster family
(Asteraceae [Compositae])

This slender, branching annual, 1–2 feet, has woolly
white leaves. Typically, the
flowers are cobalt blue, but may also be white and pink. They
bloom from May through summer. The convex solitary flower
heads are borne atop naked stalks.

Gerard called this the "Blew-Bottle or Corne Floure." Hurtsickle was another old common name for what was a pestering weed in Europe's fields of grain, blunting sickle blades at harvesttime. Long since eradicated from the English grainfield, cornflower has been a garden plant since Elizabethan days and is now known almost entirely in its cultivated forms. In the 1700s the plant had its place in colonial gardens.

Other common names are bachelor's button, bluebottle, and bluebonnet—all names applied to several other plants too. When Chiron, the centaur of Greek mythology, was pierced by Hercules's arrow, he used the plant to salve his wound—hence *Centaurea*, "centaur." *Cyanus* comes from the Greek *kyanos*, "dark blue."

THE CROCUSES

Crocus
Iris family (Iridaceae)

There are some 80 species of crocus distributed over middle and southern Europe, northern Africa, and western Asia. Some species have been cultivated throughout Europe for centuries. The name "crocus," from the Greek *krokos*, is of great antiquity, occurring in the Sanskrit and Chaldean languages. Theophrastus applied it to the saffron crocus (*C. sativus* L.), originally the most widely cultivated species, which was used by Mongols, Arabs, Greeks, and Romans as a medicine, a condiment, a disinfectant, and a dye.

DUTCH YELLOW CROCUS

C. flavus Weston
(syn. *C. aureus* Sm.)

This is probably the most widely cultivated crocus today. The 3–petaled, 3–sepaled yellow cuplike flowers open in sunshine in February and March. A white center line distinguishes the narrow leaves, which lengthen after the flower has faded.

This crocus reached England from eastern Europe before 1597. John Gerard described it as having flowers of "a most perfect shining yellow colour." *Aureus* means golden, *flavus* yellow. See illustration on p. 101.

WHITE or PURPLE DUTCH CROCUS
C. vernus Wulfen

These crocuses from southern Europe vary in the wild as they do in cultivation, the blossoms sometimes being plain, striped, or feathered. By the mid-eighteenth century, crocus corms were being imported into England from Holland in quantity, and some doubtless reached the American colonies earlier because in two letters of 1683–1684 William Byrd I wrote of crocuses. Collinson, who had "a collection as is rarely met with all at once," sent upwards of 20 different kinds to John Bartram in 1740. See illustration on p. 101.

AUTUMN CROCUS
C. kotschyanus Koch
(syn. *C. zonatus* J. Gay)

Innumerable varieties of Dutch crocuses have been developed from *C. flavus* and *C. vernus.*
Although most of the cultivated varieties flower in the spring, there are some autumn blooming kinds. Among them is this species, which grows in Colonial Williamsburg's gardens. The flowers open in September and October before the leaves appear. Varying in color from rose purple to lilac, their veined yellow throats have cream colored anthers. Native to Lebanon, this crocus is named for its discoverer, Theodor Kotschy.

CROWN IMPERIAL LILY

Fritillaria imperialis L.
Lily family (Liliaceae)

The crown imperial lily looks
like no other flower. In April
the large, dense whorl of
drooping, bell-like flowers appear brick red, orange, or yellow.
They are borne atop a stout 3–4-foot stem surmounted by a tuft
of leaves, somewhat like those of a pineapple, and have an
unpleasant, foxy scent. The seedpods, when formed, turn upward to make a perfect crown.

This is one of the oldest known cultivated plants. Native to
northern India, Persia, Afghanistan, and the Himalayas, it was
grown in Turkish gardens long before Jules Charles de L'Ecluse
sent it in 1576 from Persia to Vienna, where it first flowered in
Europe in the imperial gardens. Described as "the lily of the
turban'd countries" and as "the emperor of flowers," the plant
was given but one name—"crown imperial"—adopted by all
European languages.

Time and again Collinson sent the bulbs to Custis. Usually
they rotted during the voyage, but in 1739 Custis succeeded in
bringing one plant to flower and said that it was looked upon as
a great rarity.

Fritillaria is from the Latin *fritillus*, a checkerboard or dice-
box, because of the spot markings on the perianth of some
species.

THE DAFFODILS

Narcissus
Amaryllis family (Amaryllidaceae)

For centuries there has been confusion in the names daffodil
and narcissus. Parkinson, in 1629, complained that "many idle
and ignorant Gardeners . . . doe call some of these Daffodils

Narcissus, when as all know that know any Latine, that Narcissus is the Latin name, and Daffodil the English of one and the same things."

"Daffodil" is a variant of "affodil" (the origin of the "d" is obscure), the name that properly belonged to the white asphodel but was also given to the white, short-cupped poet's narcissus, apparently the first narcissus to be called daffodil. For a long time the small, long-trumpeted yellow narcissus (native to England, and the inspiration of Wordsworth's ode to the daffodil), was regarded as "a False or Bastard Daffodil" and was named *Narcissus pseudo-narcissus.*

Most of the 25 or 30 original species found in central Europe, the Mediterranean region, China, and Japan, are European, and all are hardy, bulbous plants. Today narcissi are defined, botanically, by 11 kinds, 4 of which are included here. *Narcissus,* the classical Latin name, from the Greek, probably alludes to the plant's narcotic qualities rather than to the youth Narcissus of mythology.

TRUMPET DAFFODILS

N. pseudo-narcissus L.

The trumpet narcissi have one flower to a stem. They are called "trumpet" daffodils on account of the length of the corona or trumpet, which distinguishes them from other narcissi species.

POET'S NARCISSUS

N. poeticus L.

These are the shallow-cupped narcissi, one flower to a stem, with the cup or corona about one-third as long as the perianth segments. All are fragrant. Included among them are the old pheasant's eye (*N. recurvus*) from Switzerland, which has backward curving segments and a yellow corona with a broad, deep red rim. This species was not brought into cultivation in England until the early nineteenth century.

POLYANTHUS NARCISSUS
N. tazetta L.

This species bears several flowers in a cluster. Its several varieties are widely distributed in southern Europe, northern Africa, and Asia Minor to China and Japan, where they have been cultivated for 3,000 years. One variety was used for funeral wreaths by the ancient Egyptians.

JONQUILS
N. jonquilla L.

Jonquils bear bunches of 2–6 short-cupped, small, golden, sweet-scented flowers on 10–

18-inch stems. They take their name from the Spanish *jonquilla*, a rush, because of their deep green rushlike leaves. Their range is wide: in Europe they are found from Spain eastward to Dalmatia, and also in Algeria.

THE DAYLILIES
Hemerocallis
Lily family (Liliaceae)

Daylilies are tuberous-rooted perennials ranging from Europe to China, where they carried the name "Plant of Forgetfulness," supposedly because they were able to cure sorrow by causing loss of memory. The Greek *hemera* and *kallow*, meaning "day" and "beautiful," refer to each flower's lasting but a single day, fading by nightfall.

COMMON ORANGE DAYLILY
H. fulva L.

The common orange daylily is a familiar garden escape in many parts of the eastern seaboard, and has become naturalized around the Capitol and across ravines in Williamsburg. In June the funnel-like reddish orange flowers open successively day by day from the buds that are grouped together at the ends of the long flower stalks. The narrow leaves mature and arch downward when the bloom is over.

    H. fulva reached England from the Levant before 1596 and is probably the name-plant of the genus. John Parkinson and Sir Thomas Hammer, another seventeenth-century flower lover, agreed that its English name, the "Lily for a Day," originated because one flower opened at a time and lasted only a day. They described its flower color as "Orange-tawny."

The tawny daylily, as it is still also called, is often—mistakenly—called "tiger lily." *Fulva* means "orange." See illustration on p. 106.

YELLOW (or LEMON) DAYLILY
H. flava L.

The yellow daylily is somewhat smaller, in both leaf and flower, than the tawny daylily. Its fragrant flowers open in May. This species reached England from Siberia before 1596. The Tatars' saddle mats were made of daylily leaves. Lady Skipwith grew both the "yellow and Tawny Day Lily." *Flava* means "yellow." See illustration on p. 106.

ENGLISH DAISY
Bellis perennis L.
Aster family
(Asteraceae [Compositae])

This little plant, widespread in Europe and Asia Minor, is the common daisy beloved by English poets. The Anglo-Saxons called it "Daezeseze." For Chaucer it was the "eye of day"; for Jonson, the "bright dayes-eyes." Elizabethan gardeners grew the double varieties. One eighteenth-century gardener listed 12 kinds, including "the double pyed quilled" and "the double speckled Coxcomb Daisy," and recommended that "the most eligible way is to plant them in rows by the side of walks." London nurserymen were by then raising "vast quantities to supply the markets in Spring." Its popularity as an edging plant has never waned.

English daisy lies low to the ground, dandelionlike, the leaves forming a basal rosette and broadening at the tips. The blooms are white or pink, red splashed or tipped; in the double varieties the central disk is almost lost among the red and white petals.

[107]

"English daisy" is the American name; bachelor's button is the name commonly given in England. *Bellis,* from the Latin "war," alludes to their supposed use on the battlefield to stanch the wounds of the fallen. *Perennis,* "perennial."

EVENING PRIMROSE, COMMON

Oenothera biennis L.
Evening Primrose family
(Onagraceae)

There are about 20 species of evening primrose, all natives to the New World. Most of them are nocturnal, as is *O. biennis,* and the flowers open at dusk. This species, found virtually throughout North America, is a biennial, 3–4 feet, branching in habit, and often producing its fragrant primrose yellow flowers the first summer. Introduced into England about 1621 and known as the primrose tree (or tree primrose) of Virginia, the plant has long since been naturalized in Britain.

   Oenothera, from the Greek *oinosthera,* means "wine-scenting" or "the pursuit of wine."

FOUR O'CLOCK

(marvel of Peru)
Mirabilis jalapa L.
Four o'clock family
(Nyctaginaceae)

Four o'clock, a herbaceous perennial, 1–2 feet, blooms profusely from late summer to fall. The long-tubed, funnel-shaped flowers, in clusters, are white, yellow, crimson, striped, or blotched, and are dustily fragrant. Native to tropical America, the plant reached England from Peru in 1596. From the first, four o'clock was regarded as an oddity among plants because the flowers open in late afternoon and close in the morning. On July 18, 1767, Jefferson wrote in his diary, "Mirabilis just opened, very clever."

Mirabilis is a shortened version of *admirabilis*, "wonderful" and "strange"; *jalapa* because it was once thought to be the source of jalap, a purgative drug obtained from a convolvulus with similar looking roots.

FOXGLOVE
Digitalis purpurea L.
Figwort or Snapdragon
family (Scrophulariaceae)

This biennial plant, native to Britain and western Europe, is now naturalized in many parts of the world. The leaves are roundish and downy. The June flowers, typically purplish pink, sometimes white, are clustered on one side of the strong 2–4-foot-tall vertical stalks. The downward slanting 2–lipped corollas, 2–3 inches long, are spotted on the inside and are bearded at the throat.

In 1748 Peter Kalm saw the plant in bloom in Philadelphia. His was the earliest known reference to the plant in America, but the chances are that it was introduced earlier.

Foxglove is from the Anglo-Saxon "Foxes-gleow," gleow being a musical instrument that consists of an arch supporting a ring of bells of graduated size. The plant had no Latin name until Leonhard Fuchs, a German physician and author of two herbals, named it *Digitalis*, "finger-flower," in 1541: "Some . . . doe call them Finger-flowers, because they are like unto the fingers of a glove, the ends cut off."

Foxglove is the source of the drug digitalis, which is used for diseases of the heart. Thirteenth-century Welsh apothecaries used the plant externally for scrofulous complaints, hence the family name.

GAILLARDIA

Gaillardia pulchella Foug.
Aster family
(Asteraceae [Compositae])

The gaillardias all belong to North America and indications are that these western plants have become naturalized in the southeastern states. *G. pulchella* (syn. *G. bicolor,* 1787) is a perennial, but is often treated as an annual. Standing erect, 12–20 inches tall, it has woolly gray leaves and red and yellow flat rayed flower heads that are yellow at the tip and rose purple at the base. Blanket flower is another common name applied to gaillardias in general. Probably it was first given to this species on account of its woolly leaves, or perhaps because the flower colors resemble the colors and patterns of Indian blankets.

It was named for Monsieur Gaillard de Marentonneau, a patron of botany in France; *pulchella* is from the Latin *pulchellus,* "pretty."

Native range: Colo. and Ariz. east to Nebr., Mo., and La. Casually as a migrant or garden escape on the Atlantic coast to Ga. and Va.

GLOBE AMARANTH

Gomphrena globosa L.
Amaranth family (Amaranthaceae)

A tender, branching annual, 2–3 feet, and a common everlasting flower, globe amaranth bears a profusion of cloverlike flowers, reddish purple, white, or pink, 1 inch or less across, from summer until frost.

The plant was brought to England from India in 1714; apparently Pennsylvania gardeners were the first in the colonies to bring the plant to bloom. Custis, who received seeds repeatedly from Collinson, wrote triumphantly to him in 1742 that one seed came up—"shot into a multitude of branches and bore more than 100 flowers; came out daily till the frost stopt them; I esteem it one of the prettyest things I ever saw." Delighted, Collinson wrote back:

> It is a Real and I may say perpetual Beauty. If the flowers are gather'd in perfection and hung up with their Heads Downwards in a Dry shady Room, they will keep thear Colours for years and will make a pleasant Ornament to Adorn the Windows of your parlor or study all the Winter. I Dry great Quantities for that purpose and putt them in flower potts and China basons and they make a fine show all the Winter.

Gomphrena is the old name for amaranth; *globosa* refers to the shape of the flower heads.

GOLDENROD, CANADA
Solidago altissima L.
(syn. *S. canadensis* L.)
Aster family
(Asteraceae [Compositae])

Most of the 125 species of goldenrod are native to North America; they are especially plentiful in the eastern states. The early flowering varieties are looked on as harbingers of fall, flowering successively from August to November.

Canada goldenrod is a stalwart perennial, 3–6 feet, and is one of the commonest species in its range. The large panicles of yellow flowers are borne in one-sided spreading or recurved racemes August to October. This was the first American species taken to England and listed by Tradescant; it has long since been naturalized there and is a parent of many modern garden hybrids.

When dry and powdered, a European species, wound-weed (*S. virgaurea*), was valued for healing wounds, being applied either externally or internally. The dried plant was imported to England and fetched a high price until its healing properties were questioned and it was found growing wild in Hampstead.

Solidago is from the Latin *solidare*, to unite or to make whole. Native range: Que. to Fla., Tex., and N. D.

GRAPE HYACINTH
Muscari botryoides (L.) Mill.
Lily family (Liliaceae)

There are about 50 species of *Muscari*, diminutive spring-flowering bulbs that are related to hyacinths and are native to the Mediterranean region. Gerard described this species as having "many little bottle-like blue flowers, closely thrust or packt together like a bunch of grapes." Parkinson called the white flowered form "Pearls of Spain." The deep blue flowers are borne in a spike of bloom at the top of a bare stalk, which at most is 12 inches high.

Muscari is from *M. moschetum*, that which has a musky scent.

GUERNSEY LILY

Nerine sarniensis (L.) Herb.
Amaryllis family
(Amaryllidaceae)

This bulb bears rose pink flowers in a close umbel on a 12–18-inch naked stem. The leaves appear after the flowers.

This nerine apparently flourished and became naturalized on the island of Guernsey in the 1600s. Sir Thomas Hammer in his *Garden Book* (1659) referred to it as "the flower of Garnsey, as wee call it," and the poet, Christopher Smart, in 1674 entitled one of his poems "On a Bed of Guernsey Lilies."

The bulb was introduced to England by 1659, possibly from Holland or Paris where it was already in cultivation, although for a long time botanists believed that the plant was native to Japan. It was later found to be indigenous to southern Africa, growing wild on Table Mountain. Collinson sent some bulbs to Custis, but there is no record of their flowering.

Nerin is the name of a sea nymph of classical mythology; *sarniensis* is the old name for the Channel Islands.

HELENIUM

(sneezeweed)
Helenium autumnale L.
Aster family
(Asteraceae [Compositae])

All 40 species of helenium, coarse annual or perennial plants that closely resemble sunflowers, are native to North America and Mexico. A leafy stemmed perennial, 4–6 feet, with oval, toothed leaves, its flower head, which is nearly 2 inches wide, has light yellow, drooping, 3–clefted rays and a darker yellow disk. This is one of the commonest heleniums in cultivation, and many garden forms with yellow and crimson rays have been developed from it.

Helenium is from an ancient Greek name that Hippocrates used for a plant; *autumnale* refers to its flowering season (August–November).

Native range: Que. to Fla. and Ariz.

HOLLYHOCK

Althaea rosea Cav.
Mallow family (Malvaceae)

The hollyhock is native to China and was in cultivation there for several centuries before it became a familiar plant in English gardens, and was grown for a time as a florists' flower. "Holy-Hoc" (*hoc* was the Anglo-Saxon word for mallow) underscores the tradition that the plant was brought to England at the time of the Crusades. However, it may not have been established in cultivation until it was reintroduced from the Orient in 1573.

Hollyhock is a biennial. The flowers, in July-August, are pink, white, red, and pale yellow, 3 inches or more across, and are clustered along the 6–9-foot spirelike stems.

The single varieties, white, pink, and red, appeared in the early colonists' gardens. John Josselyn noted the plants when he was in New England, and his may be the earliest reference to the hollyhock in America. One English gardener thought the plant "fittest for courts or spatious gardens, being so great and stately," while another, John Lawrence, suggested in 1726 that the "Proper Places against walls or the Corners of Gardens should be assigned to them, where they may explain their Beauty to distant view."

Althaea is the Greek for the marsh mallow (*A. officinalis*); *rosea*, rose colored.

HYACINTH, COMMON

Hyacinthus orientalis L.
Lily family (Liliaceae)

Hyacinth's fragrant, recurving, bell-like flowers—white and various shades of pink and blue—are clustered on stout 8–18-inch-high stalks.

The bulb was cultivated in England before 1576. Sir Thomas More, in *A Flower Garden for Gentlemen and Ladies* (1734), explained how the flowers could be forced into early bloom. If grown on perforated corks and set in windows, they would bloom in winter and so "supply the curious Ladies . . . with Nosegays to adorn their Bosom at Christmas."

Hyacinths, both single and double, were among the flowers grown by the early colonists. In 1688 John Banister recorded seeing them in Virginia. Richard Stockton, a future signer of the Declaration of Independence, wrote to his wife that she already had "as fine tulips and hyacinths . . . as any in England, yet I shall order some of the finest."

Hyacinthus is the early Greek name for this long cultivated plant; *orientalis* means of Near East origin.

THE IRISES

Iris
Iris family (Iridaceae)

The iris is one of the oldest cultivated plants. The Egyptians, who probably obtained the plant from Syria, used it to adorn the brows of statues of the Sphinx. Many centuries later it appeared as the *fleur-de-lis* on the royal arms of France and Britain.

The genus comprises some 200 species of perennial plants that grow from rhizomes or bulbs. Native to the north temperate zones, many species occur in North America. Innumerable irises are in cultivation; those included here are grown in Colonial Williamsburg's Historic Area.

Theophrastus named the genus for Iris, the Greek goddess of the rainbow.

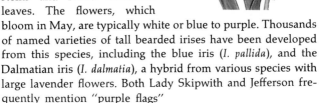

GERMAN IRIS
I. germanica L.

This iris has stout 2–4-foot stems and broad swordlike leaves. The flowers, which bloom in May, are typically white or blue to purple. Thousands of named varieties of tall bearded irises have been developed from this species, including the blue iris (*I. pallida*), and the Dalmatian iris (*I. dalmatia*), a hybrid from various species with large lavender flowers. Both Lady Skipwith and Jefferson frequently mention "purple flags" and "Common Blue."

SIBERIAN IRIS
I. sibirica L.

The Siberian iris, with grassy leaves, grows its blue, purple, and lavender flowers on

2–4-foot stems in May. It was grown in England before 1596, having been introduced from central Europe and Russia.

YELLOW FLAG
(water flag)
I. pseudacorus L.

This water loving iris has glaucous, 1–inch-wide leaves, and
clustered bright yellow flowers
on 2–3-foot stems in May and June. Early writers recognized
that the yellow flag was not a lily, but it is generally accepted as
the origin of the *fleur-de-lis* and was known by that name until
the eighteenth century. These "lilies" of France were incorporated in the royal arms of Great Britain in 1340; in 1800 they
were displaced to make room for the Irish harp. It is native to
Europe and Britain.

THE LARKSPURS
Delphinium
Buttercup family (Ranunculaceae)

Larkspurs belong to a genus of about 100 species of annual,
biennial, or perennial plants native to Europe, Asia, and North
America. Larkspurs are among the annuals. The name "larkspur" refers to the spur-shaped nectary that perhaps resembles
the spur on the foot of a lark. *Delphinium,* the Greek name of
one species, was used by Dioscorides; Gerard thought it referred to the flower's resemblance to the fabled dolphin, pic-
tured "with a crooked and bending figure of shape."

COMMON LARKSPUR
D. consolida L.

Also known as garden larkspur, this European species was a familiar of the early colonial garden. It is an annual or biennial with a 2–3-foot branching stem and delicately serrate leaves. The flowers in June–July are typically azure blue, rarely rose or white. It is a parent of today's branching larkspurs.

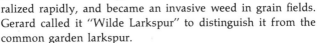

ROCKET LARKSPUR
D. ajacis L.

Native to Europe, rocket larkspur was brought to England in the sixteenth century, naturalized rapidly, and became an invasive weed in grain fields. Gerard called it "Wilde Larkspur" to distinguish it from the common garden larkspur.

By 1659 there were some 9 colors of rocket larkspurs in single, double, and variegated forms. Bartram experimented in hybridizing larkspur types. Wrote Collinson: "I am delighted with his operation on the larkspur. The product is wonderful. If these charming flowers can be continued by seed, they will be the greatest ornament of the garden." The rocket larkspur is the parent of today's rocket or single stemmed larkspur varieties.

THE LILIES
Lilium
Lily family (Liliaceae)

Lilies include about 80 species of bulbous plants and are native to the temperate regions of the northern hemisphere. *Lilium*, the old Latin name, is akin to the Greek *Leirion* used by Theophrastus for the madonna lily.

MADONNA LILY
L. candidum L.

In June the madonna lily opens its clear waxy white trumpet-shaped flowers with slightly recurved petals and yellow anthers. Several to many blooms are borne in close erect racemes on stiff straight stems, 2–4 feet tall.

This may be the oldest domesticated flower and is one of the most common hardy outdoor white lilies today. It was known in the eastern Mediterranean 3,000 years before Christ. The Cretans and Egyptians used the root for medicinal purposes, while the Romans, who probably brought the plant to Britain, used the juice of the root or an ointment made from it to cure corns. Queen Elizabeth's sergeant-surgeon believed that the root dipped in honey would "cure burnings and scaldings without a scar, and trimly deck a blank place with hair."

For centuries painters depicted the lily in paintings of the Virgin Mary, the tradition being that three days after burial, her tomb was found empty save for lilies and roses. Yet only in the nineteenth century was the name "Madonna" applied. Up to that time the plant was known as the white lily, which is how Lady Skipwith listed it.

CANADA LILY
(wild yellow, or meadow lily)
L. canadense L.

Meadow lily has nodding yellow flowers with chocolate spotted throats and yellow anthers. Three to 15 blooms are carried on the 2–5-foot stalks in midsummer.

This is one of the most widely distributed lilies of eastern North America and, introduced by the French about 1620, was the first American lily to become known in Europe. Parkinson described it in his *Paradisus* (1629). The Canada lily was frequently called martagon from the eighteenth century onward. Mark Catesby made a striking portrait of it for his *Natural History* and called it "Martagon Canadense, Le Lis de Canada or Martagon. These plants were produced from scaly roots sent from Pensylvania, and have flowered several years in Mr. Collinson's garden at Peckham." Lady Skipwith listed it as the "Spotted Canada Martagon Lily." Canada lily is distinguished by the petals that flare out like bells; those of the true martagon are recurved.

Native range: Que. and N. S., S. C., Ala., Ky., and Minn.

Martagons were very popular in the eighteenth century, when few other lilies were known. The true martagon or Turks-cap lily (*L. martagon* L.) has nodding, strongly recurved, thickly spotted flowers varying in color from orange to yellow and red. It was widely cultivated and was also grown as a pot plant in spite of its disagreeable scent. It was easy to grow and bloomed in early summer.

The American Turks-cap lily or tiger lily is the European martagon's splendid counterpart. Growing up to 8 feet, it carries as many as 40 long-stalked, pendulous, maroon dotted blooms that vary in color from orange to crimson. "This stately Martagon," as Collinson called it, flowered in his garden in 1738 from bulbs sent him by

Bartram. In 1762 Linnaeus named it *superbum,* superb.
Native range: N. B. to Ga., Mo., and Minn.

THE LOBELIAS
Lobelia
Bellflower family (Campanulaceae [including Lobeliaceae])

Some 250 species of these annual or perennial plants are found in many parts of the world. It was named for Matthias de L'Obel, botanist-physician to James I.

BLUE LOBELIA
L. siphilitica L.

Blue lobelia is a strong, weedy perennial, 2–3 feet, with deep blue or violet purple flowers carried on a long, wandlike raceme. Linnaeus named the plant *siphilitica* because Kalm reported that the Indians used a decoction of the plant as a remedy for that venereal desease.
Native range: Me. to Tex., Kans., and Minn.

CARDINAL FLOWER
L. cardinalis L.

Few historians have concerned themselves about ornamental plants, but Robert Beverley,

Virginia's first historian, did. He wrote: "Of spontaneous Flowers they have an unknown Variety: the finest Crown Imperial in the World; the Cardinal Flower, so extoll'd for its Scarlet Colour, is almost in every Branch." (Branch means a creek or inlet.)

This perennial, which grows up to 4 feet, bears flowers on a 1-sided leafy raceme; each flower has a cleft, 2-lipped, scarlet corolla. According to Parkinson, it was first introduced to Europe from the French colony in Canada. The story goes that Henrietta Maria, queen of England, laughed exceedingly when she saw the flower, saying that the color reminded her of the scarlet stockings worn by cardinals. However that may be, the color matches that of a cardinal's rich crimson robes, and from the first the plant was known as the cardinal flower.

Native range: N. B. to Fla., Tex., and Minn.

LOVE LIES BLEEDING
Amaranthus caudatus L.
Amaranthus family
(Amaranthaceae)

This tender annual, some 3 feet high, blooms all summer. Its countless tiny purplish red flowers are densely clustered in long downward pointing spires. It reached England from the Tropics about 1596. Gerard and Parkinson knew it as Great Purple Flower-Gentle. In 1665 John Rea said, "This is an old flower and commonly called by some Country women, Love lies a-bleeding." The plant was known in the American colonies by the 1700s.

Amaranthus is from the Greek *a*, "not," and *maraino*, "to wither"—"unfading," "never-waxing-old." The name was given to a plant or plants with flower parts that retain their form and color for a long time. Thus the word "amaranth" signified immortality, and English poets since Milton have used amaranth, amaracus, and amaranthine with much poetic license.

Botanists have been less enamored of the name. They have

reclassified plants that were once included in the genus *Amaranthus,* although they still belong to the amaranth family. The globe amaranth that Philip Miller, Peter Collinson, and others called *amaranthoides* now goes by the ugly name *Gomphrena globosa,* although in all fairness it was Pliny who used the name *Gomphrena* for some kind of amaranth. Those cockscombs with feathery plumes that were dried for winter decoration are now called *Celosia.*

Love lies bleeding is the only true "everlasting" in cultivation in the genus *Amaranthus.*

TWO MARIGOLDS

Tagetes
Aster family (Asteraceae [Compositae])

Common names can be misleading. Marigold (*Calendula officinalis*) is generally known in America as calendula and is therefore listed under that name in this handbook. Calendulas belong to the Old World; the French and African marigolds, native neither to France nor to Africa but to Mexico, belong to a different New World genus, *Tagetes. Tagetes* perhaps was named for Tages, an Etruscan god.

AFRICAN MARIGOLD

T. erecta L.

A vigorous, stout, erect, branching annual, to 2 feet, with solitary yellow or deep orange flower heads, it blooms from June to October. Brought to Spain from Mexico and called Rose of the Indies, the plant was naturalized along the North African coast and became accepted as a local flower. Reintroduced into Europe and to England (1596), it was known as *Flos Africanus,* a compliment to Emperor Charles V, who freed Tunis from the Moors (1535).

The name continued into the eighteenth century and *Flos Africanus* was accepted as an ornamental, although, in the opinion of the Reverend William Hanbury, author of *A Complete Body of Planting and Gardening* (1770): "These flowers stink as bad, or worse, than the French Marygolds, though there is a variety of it that is tolerably sweet-scented, on which account many are curious in collecting the seeds." Parkinson described the scent of the double flower as "the very smell of new waxe, or of an honie combe, and not of the poisonful sent of the smaller kindes." Thomas Fairchild recommended both French and African marigolds for London gardens.

Erecta is the Latin for "upright."

FRENCH MARIGOLD
T. patula L.

French marigold was known in England by 1573. It is a small compact plant about 9 inches high, whose small yellow or orange crinkled flower heads, marked red or brown, bloom from June to October. On March 1, 1793, Sir Peyton Skipwith bought "striped French Marygold" from Minton Collins of Richmond, Virginia. *Patula* is from the Latin *patulus*, "slightly spreading."

NASTURTIUM
Tropaeolum majus L.
Nasturtium family
(Tropaeolaceae)

Nasturtium is an old favorite that is useful as well as decorative. The rounded leaves are carried on long leaf stalks. The spurred, trumpetlike flowers, 2½ inches across, come in clear bright yellow, orange, and red, and bloom from midsummer until frost. Both flowers and leaves may be used in salads, and the young green seed pods can be pickled as a substitute for capers. In his *Treatise on Gardening,* John Randolph wrote: "It is thought the flower is superior to a radish in flavour, and is eat in salads, or *without.*" At Monticello, Jefferson set his "Nasturtiums in 35 little hills." The dwarf nasturtium (*T. minus*) reached England from Peru first; the larger species (*T. majus*) followed in 1686.

Tropaeolum refers to an ancient custom. After a battle victorious armies chose a tree or set up a tall trophy pole, the *tropaeum,* on which the armor and equipment of the vanquished foe was draped as an emblem of victory. The red and yellow flowers reminded Linnaeus of the blood-stained helmets of the fallen, and the rounded leaves of shields. Nasturtium can be translated as "nose tormentor" on account of the peppery taste of the leaves, which resembles that of watercress, then known as *Nasturtium officinale.* Indian cress, another common name, refers to the time of its introduction into Europe—Spanish territories in South America were known by the general name of "the Indies."

NIGELLA
(fennel flower)
Nigella damascena L.
Buttercup family
(Ranunculaceae)

Fairchild, a notable English nurseryman, thought nigella "rather an odd Plant, than beautiful in its Flowers; for the Blossom is of a very pale blue Colour, and is encompass'd with shagged Leaves, as if was t'yd up in a Bunch of Fewel [possibly a misprint for fennel]." His description fits this hardy annual well. It grows 1–2 feet and has bright green, finely cut leaves and blue flowers within a whorl of threadlike bracts.

Brought to England from the Mediterranean region about 1570, Gerard knew it as nigella, Parkinson as fennel flower. Devil-in-a-bush, one of several other common names, appeared in 1722. When love-in-a-mist came into use is not known, but the plant still goes by that name in England today.

Nigella refers to the small black 3–cornered seeds; *damascena* because at the time of its introduction it was thought to have come from Damascus.

PANSY
Viola tricolor L.
Violet family (Violaceae)

This is the original pansy, the small-flower species "of three sundrie colours . . . , that is to say purple, yellow and white or blewe." So Gerard described the little flowers with black markings—said to be guidelines for insects—and a patch or blotch on the lower petals. This wild pansy, native to England, Europe, and Asia, is an annual or short-lived perennial that reseeds itself readily. Cultivated from medieval times, some of its many folk names include wild pansy, heartsease, love-in-idleness, three faces in a hood, tittle-my-fancy, call-me-to-you, kiss-me-by-the-garden-gate, and Johnny-jump-up. North America's only native pansy (*V. ratinesquil*) is commonly known as Johnny-jump-up.

The hybrid pansies and violas of today originated in the nineteenth century and are very unlike *V. tricolor*. It was around 1812 that Lady Mary Bennet and her gardener, Richardson, and Lord Gambier and his gardener, Thompson, began to cultivate and improve *V. tricolor* and *V. lutea*, along with other native species. Mr. Thompson, as he is referred to, became known as the father of the heartsease. Jefferson grew "tricolor" at Monticello.

The common name comes from *pensée*, the French for thought; *viola* is the Latin for violet.

PEONY, COMMON

Paeonia officinalis L.
Buttercup family
(Ranunculaceae)

Common peony (also spelled
paeony) is a hardy, long-lived,
and handsomely leafy herba-
ceous perennial some 2 feet in height. The leaves are compound, the leaflets deeply cut. The solitary dark crimson or
white flowers, 5 inches across, grow on strong single stems in
April and May.

Pliny said that the peony, native to southern Europe and
western Asia, was one of the oldest cultivated plants. The
common peony and the tree peony (*P. suffruticosa*) have been
cultivated in China since "time immemorial" and are part of its
history and symbolism. Both sorts were cultivated in Japan by
the eighth century.

The double crimson peony was brought to England from the
Mediterranean region before 1548. The double white, although
in cultivation in Europe, reached England sometime later; Gerard hoped to get it from "the low countries of Flaunders."
Peony roots were a supposed cure for "the falling sickness" and
were hung around the necks of children as a preventative.
According to John Hill, the common peony was neglected by
eighteenth-century gardeners: "If new brought from *America*,
the whole Botanic World would resound with its praise." (His
remark reveals the Old World's intense interest in New World
plants.)

Paeonia, the ancient Greek name used by Theophrastus, is
said to be derived from Paeon, the physician who first used the
plant medicinally.

PERIWINKLE

Vinca minor L.
Oleander family
(Apocynaceae)

Periwinkle is a familiar
groundcover plant, a creeping
evergreen with lance-shaped,
shining leaves and solitary blue flowers in April and May.
Native to Europe, it was probably brought to Britain by the
Romans.

There is no known reason why "pervink," from the old Latin
name *Vinca pervinca,* was corrupted to the name the plant
shares with the periwinkle, a shellfish. *Vinca,* from the Latin
vincula, "a band," was applied to *V. major* L., a plant similar to
but larger than *V. minor. V. major* was commonly called band-
plant and cut-finger, as it was believed that a band of periwinkle tied around the calf of the leg eased cramp and that the
leaves, when chewed, stopped bleeding from the nose or
mouth.

PHLOX, SUMMER

Phlox paniculata L.
Phlox family
(Polemoniaceae)

The phloxes are all native to
North America except for one
Asiatic species. Summer phlox
is a stout, erect perennial, 2–4 feet or more high, with tapering
leaves. The flowers, in a pyramidal panicle, are pink purple in
summer and early autumn. The plant was introduced into

England from the southern colonies and was recorded as flowering first in 1732. Collinson described it in 1744 as "a new lychnidea, sent by J. Bartram with a large spike of pale reddish purple flowers, with peach-shaped leaves." *P. paniculata* is a parent of the common perennial phloxes of today's gardens, which have developed in many colors—white, salmon, rose, scarlet, lilac, magenta, and purple. In the evening phlox is strongly and sweetly scented.

Phlox was a name used by Theophrastus for a plant with flame-colored flowers; *paniculata* means panicled.

Native range: N. Y. to Ga., Ark., and Kans.

THE PINKS
Dianthus
Pink family (Caryophyllaceae)

The pink has been called the poor man's carnation, and there is a vast literature about the two closely allied species of *Dianthus*. Pinks were the favorite flower of Queen Henrietta Maria, the wife of Charles I. Many types of pinks, in a wide color range and richly fragrant, were developed during the reigns of the Stuarts, including some with jagged and fringed flowers and a single form with an "eye," a circular band of color around the center of the flower. Laced pinks were known by 1750, and 20 years later, the weavers of Lancashire brought the laced-pink type to perfection. Toward the end of the century, artisan-florists—coalminers and weavers—brought the laced pinks and the eye-pinks to perfection.

From the sixteenth to the eighteenth centuries the word "pink" was used as a synonym for the "flower of excellence"—hence "the pink of perfection" and the colloquialism "in the pink." Not until later was "pink" used as a color name.

Dianthus from the Greek *dios* and *anthos*, "divine" and "flower," the name given the genus by Theophrastus in allusion to the fragrance and color of the flower of many species.

THE PINK

(grass pink)
D. plumarius L.

D. plumarius is one of the principal ancestors of today's garden pinks (hence *the* pink). It is
a low growing plant with slender pale blue green leaves and
white or rose pink fringed flowers in May and June. Native to
southern Europe, it was in cultivation in England by 1578,
perhaps much earlier. *Plumarius* means "feathered."

CHINESE PINK

D. chinensis L.

Chinese or Indian pink is a
perennial, 12–18 inches, with
bright to dull red or white
flowers from June to September. Native to eastern Asia, its
seeds were sent to England by a member of the East India
Company in 1716. By the mid-eighteenth century both single
and double forms were grown in English gardens in many
shades and colors.

Lady Skipwith's flower list included "Pinks of Various kinds,
very fine Chinese Pink, Double and Single." Custis grew "Indian pinks" and probably got the seed from John Bartram, as
Collinson suggested he might do in a letter of January 1736/37:
"If you have any Correspondents in Philadelphia there is Two
of my Friends viz Doctor Witt att German Town and John

Bartram on Skulkill both places near Philadelphia, these Friends of mine have gott from France the Double Flowering China or India pink. If you send to Either of them in my Name I doubt not by they'l readly send you some seed."

Some reference should be made to the clove-scented carnation, *D. caryophyllus* L. It is a very old garden plant. Pliny wrote that the plant was discovered in Spain in the time of Augustus Caesar and that the Spaniards used it as a spicy flavoring in summer drinks. This use persisted down through the centuries. One English name for the carnation was sops-in-wine; another was gillyflower, a name perhaps derived from July-flower or *jolie-fleur*. Thomas Glover, in his *Account of Virginia* (1676), noted "clove-gilliflowers" in planters' gardens.

The carnation was and still is, in both the old and modern sense of the phrase, a florists' flower. Today it is grown chiefly as a greenhouse plant.

POPPY ANEMONE

Anemone coronaria L.
Buttercup family
(Ranunculaceae)

Poppy anemone's stalked leaves are cut into deeply toothed segments, a beautiful,
delicate, early spring foliage. The poppylike flowers, solitary on smooth stalks, 10–18 inches, open in April and May in rich shades of red, blue, violet, saffron yellow, or white.

Native to southern Europe and central Asia, it was known in England by 1596. Poppy anemone was a popular garland flower with the Greeks and the Romans and was the parent-in-chief of the many colored spring anemones praised by Parkinson. Gerard said that he had 12 different sorts in his garden, "and yet I do heare of divers more . . . every new year bringeth with it new, and strange kinds. . . ." In 1659 Sir Thomas Hammer listed over 50 named varieties. Today the St. Brigid anemone, one of the best known garden varieties, is the one sold by florists. A tuberous-rooted plant, commercial cultivation is confined to California and the South; it thrives in Williamsburg, but is not reliable farther north.

Anemone from the classical Greek name for "windflower"; *coronaria*, "garland."

RANUNCULUS

Ranunculus asiaticus L.
Buttercup family
(Ranunculaceae)

The garden ranunculus grows
1–2 feet, is sparingly branched,
and has compound buttercup-
like leaves. The double flowers, predominantly orange and yellow, are borne on long stalks, with 1–4 on a stem.

Native to southeastern Europe and southwestern Asia, the corms were imported from Turkey to Europe in the sixteenth century. Two forms emerged in cultivation: the turban, and the Persian king-cup or buttercup. Both became florists' flowers. At the peak of the ranunculus rage (1760–1770) it was estimated that there were more varieties of ranunculus than of any other flower.

Ranunculus is the diminutive of *rana*, a frog, referring to the watery habitat of some species; *asiaticus*, Asiatic in origin.

ROSE MALLOW

Hibiscus moscheutos L.
Mallow family (Malvaceae)

Rose mallow is a handsome
plant growing to 8 feet and
found in brackish and fresh-

water marshes from Maryland to Alabama. The sparse 5-petaled cream colored flowers with a red or purple eye are 4–8 inches across and bloom in July and August. *Hibiscus* is the ancient Greek name for the marsh mallow, and probably is derived from the ibis, the long-billed wading bird held sacred by the Egyptians, either because the ibis fed on the plant or because the seed pods of many species are like the bird's bill—long, pointed, and curved. *Moscheutos* was Linnaeus's version of the herbalists' name for a plant that they believed to be the plant Pliny called *Rosa moscheutos.*

The marsh mallow proper (*Althaea officinalis*), native to Britain and Europe, was surely brought to the American colonies early; it has long since been an "escape" in salt- or freshwater marshes from Quebec to Virginia and other scattered places inland. The plant used to be cultivated for its mucilaginous roots from which marshmallow was obtained; it has been replaced by a synthetic mixture of various sugars and gelatin.

Native range: Md. to Fla., Tex., and Ind.

SNAPDRAGON

(antirrhinum)
Antirrhinum majus L.
Figwort family
(Scrophulariaceae)

Snapdragon, a perennial usually grown as an annual, is a
branched plant that grows to
1–3 feet. The early summer flowers, in close racemes, come in various colors and color combinations and bloom again in the autumn if the old flower-spikes are cut off. Each flower is tubular; the upper lip is erect, and the lower has a large bearded palate. The corolla is closed at the mouth. Bees and other insects in search of pollen sometimes push their way too deeply into the corolla and the mouth shuts behind them, trapping them within—hence "snapdragon."

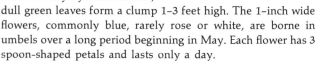

SPIDERWORT

Tradescantia virginiana L.
Spiderwort family
(Commelinaceae)

This hardy herbaceous plant
shares certain characteristics
with the daylily. The narrow,
dull green leaves form a clump 1–3 feet high. The 1–inch wide
flowers, commonly blue, rarely rose or white, are borne in
umbels over a long period beginning in May. Each flower has 3
spoon-shaped petals and lasts only a day.

Spiderwort was thought to be a cure for the bite of a poisonous spider that later proved to be harmless. Trinity-flower was
another name for the 3–petaled flower. Parkinson wrote in 1629
of *Tradescantia virginiana*, "The soon-fading Spiderwort of Virginia, or Tradescant his Spiderwort." John Tradescant the Elder
received the plant from a friend "who brought it out of Virginia."

The family name, Commelinaceae, is a prime example of
Linnaeus's flair for giving plants appropriate names. He explained, "Commelina has flowers with three petals, two of
which are showy, while the third is not conspicuous: two botanists called Commelin were noteworthy, the third died before
accomplishing anything in botany."

Native range: Me. to Ga., Ark.,
Wis., and Pa.

STAR OF BETHLEHEM

Ornithogalum umbellatum L.
Lily family (Liliaceae)

This bulb bears short-stalked
clusters of 10–20 small white
flowers, which are striped

green on the underside, in May. Usually the flowers open around 11 A.M. and close at 3, but only when the sun is shining.

Among the many folk names are eleven o'clock (in English, French, and Italian), wake-at-noon, and sleepy dick. The plant reached England from Europe and northern Africa by the sixteenth century, and was introduced into the American colonies in the 1700s. Bartram obtained his bulbs from Collinson in 1740.

The genus name stems from the Greek *ornis*, "bird," and *gala*, "milk." Why it was so named is not known. *Umbellatum* in Latin means "shadow" or "small umbrella."

DROOPING STAR OF BETHLEHEM

O. nutans L.

This *ornithogalum* is a far more distinctive plant than its namesake. The Quaker gray and white flowers, jade striped, bloom in April and May. They are 1 inch long, blunt, and droop in a loose, 3–12-flowered, 1–sided raceme that is 8–12 inches long. Native to southern Europe, the plant naturalized in Britain but is now rare there in the wild. Both species are cultivated in Williamsburg gardens and grow wild in the vicinity.

Nutans, "nodding."

STERNBERGIA

Sternbergia lutea
(L.) Sprengel
Amaryllis family
(Amaryllidaceae)

Sternbergia is a bulbous plant with narrow leaves and solitary, crocuslike, glistening yellow flowers that resemble the crocus in form and appear in August and September. The plant is sometimes called fall daffodil, but it resembles the daffodil in color only. It was introduced into England from the Mediterranean region before 1596. Lady Skipwith listed it as "yellow Autumn Amaryllis-Daffodil."

Sternbergia commemorates Count Caspar Sternberg (1761–1838) of Austria, writer, botanist, and founder of the Bohemian National Museum in Prague. *Lutea* is yellow in Latin.

SWEET WILLIAM
Dianthus barbatus L.
Pink family
(Caryophyllaceae)

Sweet William is an annual with erect stems that grows 12–24 inches high. The com-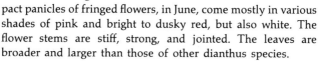pact panicles of fringed flowers, in June, come mostly in various shades of pink and bright to dusky red, but also white. The flower stems are stiff, strong, and jointed. The leaves are broader and larger than those of other dianthus species.

This is a very old garden plant that is native to southern Europe and perhaps was introduced into England by Carthusian monks in the twelfth century. Quantities were planted in Henry VIII's new garden at Hampton Court. There are various (unexplained) traditions for the name sweet William; bloomy-downs, expressive of the bunched flower heads, was one old common name.

Gerard wrote: "These plants are not used either in meate or medicine, but esteemed for their beautie to decke up gardens, the bosomes of the beautiful, garlands and crownes for pleasure." Fairchild, one of the first to make experiments in artificial hybridization (although he regarded it as unnatural and immoral), tried crossing the sweet William with the carnation. The cross became known as Fairchild's "mule." Sweet William was growing in colonial gardens by the mid-1700s. Minton Collins of Richmond had the seed; so did Lady Skipwith and Jefferson.

Dianthus is from the Greek *dios*, "divine," plus *anthos*, "flower," the name given to the genus by Theophrastus; *barbatus*, "bearded," refers to the usually bearded lower surface of the petals.

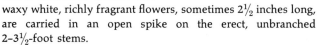

TUBEROSE

Polianthes tuberosa L.
Amaryllis family
(Amaryllidaceae)

The tuberose grows from a bulb-shaped rootstock or tuber and is classed as a bulb. The waxy white, richly fragrant flowers, sometimes $2\frac{1}{2}$ inches long, are carried in an open spike on the erect, unbranched 2–$3\frac{1}{2}$-foot stems.

Native to Mexico, the plant was introduced into England before 1629 and was highly prized by eighteenth-century gardeners. Collinson sent Custis a supply, and he was surprised that Custis "had them not, when they are on both sides of you in south Carolina and Pensilvania, my friend from Last place writ Me he had last years 149 flowers on one single Flower Stalk which is very Extriordinary but I have heard the Like from Carolina where they Stand in the Ground and Increase amazeingly."

Custis reported the following year that they "all came up and blowed well." Later when Collinson asked whether he needed a further supply, Custis replied, "I can raise them in plenty here they being of a great encrease and agree with the country very well."

Polianthes is probably from *polios*, "white," and *anthos*, "flower."

TULIP
Tulipa
Lily family (Liliaceae)

More than 150 species of tulips are native to the Mediterranean region, western and central Asia, and northern Africa. De Busbecq, the ambassador of the Holy Roman Empire to Suleiman the Magnificent, saw the garden tulip on his way to Constantinople in 1554 and brought some bulbs back to Vienna in 1572. Tulip bulbs reached England from Vienna. In 1582 Richard Hakluyt, the British geographer and chronicler of voyages of discovery, said, "Within these four years there have been brought into England from Vienna in Austria diverse kinds of flowers called Tulipes. . . ."

The tulip had been grown in Turkish gardens and as a "Royal Flower" long before the Turkish tulip epoch (1700–1730), when 1,232 varieties were listed. In 1574, Selim II ordered 50,000 bulbs for his royal gardens. The rage for tulips in Holland, now referred to as "tulipomania," reached its peak 1634–1637. All Dutchmen, rich and poor alike, speculated in tulip bulbs, and some changed hands for fantastic sums. Valuable tulip bulbs were sometimes eaten by accident or in ignorance—ironically, in World War II, the Dutch ate tulip bulbs to eke out their food supply. When the market in tulip bulbs finally crashed—it did so almost overnight—the event was recognized as a national disaster. England, too, speculated in tulips, but never to excess, as occurred in Holland.

Tulips that are all of one color, which are known as "selfs" or "breeders," may be divided, as are no other flowers, into striped, flaked, flamed, feathered, and variously marbled forms. Therein lay their fascination for the speculator and the florist—and for the early Dutch and Flemish flower painters. Up to the end of the nineteenth century the florists' tulip in England meant only the May-flowering, self-colored, cup-shaped flowers with no color other than white or yellow in the base of the bloom. Today many other forms are recognized and defined.

Tulipa comes from the oriental word for turban.

VIRGINIA BLUEBELLS

Mertensia virginica (L.) Persoon
Borage family (Boraginaceae)

This is one of North America's
lovely woodlanders, a perennial plant, 1–2 feet, with
strongly veined leaves and clusters of nodding, trumpet-shaped blue flowers that open from pink buds in early spring. Eighteenth-century gardeners in England and Virginia knew *M. virginica* as the Virginia cowslip or Roanoke bells. Custis, in his first known letter to Collinson, referred to it as "mountain cowslip," and Collinson in later correspondence spoke of it as "Your pretty Mountain blew Cowslip."

In the 1754 abridged edition of his *Gardener's Dictionary*, Miller says that the seeds of *M. virginica* were originally sent by Banister to Bishop Compton and "some other Curious Persons." Plants raised from this seed eventually died out. Collinson, in a memorandum of 1765, stated that this "most elegant plant was entirely lost in our gardens, but I again restored it from Virginia by Col. Custis, flowered April 13, 1747, and hath continued ever since a great ornament in my gardens at Mill Hill."

The genus was named for Karl Mertens, a German botanist (1764–1831).

Native range: Me. to Ga., Ark., and Minn.

YARROW

(milfoil)
Achillea millefolium L.
Aster family
(Asteraceae [Compositae])

Common yarrow is a mat-forming
plant, 1–3 feet, with leaves deeply
cut in narrow segments and small
white flowers clustered in nearly flat flower heads.

Cultivated in England before 1440, the herb had many uses.
Its green leaves were chewed to ease toothache and migraine
headaches. Gerard maintained that it was often found growing
in churchyards to reproach the dead, who would not be there
had they taken yarrow daily while alive. Sneeze-wort was
another common name for this plant because since ancient
times another species, *A. ptarmica* (from a Greek word meaning
"sneeze-making"), had been used as a kind of snuff.

Native to Europe and Asia, yarrow has long been extensively
naturalized in North America. William Wood, who traveled in
New England (1629–1633), saw "perennial yarrow" in planted
gardens; Kalm noticed it in Philadelphia and Montreal.

Yarrow is from the Anglo-Saxon name *Geawre;* milfoil and
millefolium (from the Norman *millefeuille*) were the herbalists'
names for the leaves when finely cut into innumerable parts.
Achillea is after Achilles, who is said to have discovered its
virtues in healing by using it to
stanch his soldiers' wounds.

YORKTOWN ONION

Allium ampeloprasum L.
Lily family (Liliaceae)

Yorktown onion is a purely
local name for the wild leek of
Europe that grows along the

Colonial Parkway and on the Yorktown battlefield. This *Allium* has numerous bulblets inside the papery coat. The round, dark purple, many flowered heads are 2–5 inches across atop a 3–6-foot stem. Today the flower heads are smaller and the stems are shorter than in the 1930s, due perhaps to constant mowing.

The wild leek of southern Europe and western Asia has naturalized far and wide; it has been found in the wild from Britain eastward to the Caucasus and Iran, southward to northern Africa, and in scattered areas in Virginia and the Carolinas. It is the ancestor of the cultivated leek (*A. porrum* L.), which has been grown for centuries, certainly since the time of the ancient Egyptians and in Britain since Saxon times. How the plant came to the southeastern states is not known, but probably it was mixed in fodder in colonial days. It would hardly have been brought in to be grown for food when the cultivated leek was so well known.

Allium is the ancient Latin name for garlic. The genus includes the onion, chives, leeks, and garlic.

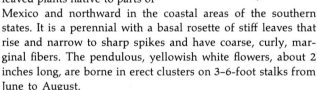

YUCCA, ADAM'S NEEDLE
Yucca filamentosa L.
Lily family (Liliaceae)

This is one of about 30 species of Yucca, which are bayonet-leaved plants native to parts of Mexico and northward in the coastal areas of the southern states. It is a perennial with a basal rosette of stiff leaves that rise and narrow to sharp spikes and have coarse, curly, marginal fibers. The pendulous, yellowish white flowers, about 2 inches long, are borne in erect clusters on 3–6-foot stalks from June to August.

In September 1585 Thomas Hariot found the plant on the islands of the North Carolina Outer Banks. He was the first Englishman to describe it:

Silk of grass, or grass silk. There is a kind of grass in this country, upon the blades whereof there grows very good silk in the form of a thin glittering skin to be strip off. It grows two feet and a half high, or better: the blades are about two feet in length and half an inch broad. The like grows in Persia, which is in the self same climate as Virginia, of which very many of the silk works that come from there into Europe, are made.

The Indians used the marginal fibers for making cloth until about 1748, when cloth became available from Europe. Sailors' hammocks were probably so called after the "hamacks" the Indians wove from yucca cordage. John Bartram sent "silk Grass" to Collinson in 1735, and George Washington grew the plant experimentally.

Y. filamentosa flowered in England in 1675, when it was known by the name Hariot gave it, silk grass, for the threads that hang from the leaf-margins. Gerard mistakenly believed the plant to be the *yuca*, the Carib name for *Manihot utilissima*, the Brazilian arrowroot or tapioca plant. Although Thomas Johnson made a correction in the revised 1635 edition of Gerard's herbal, a correction upheld by Parkinson in his *Theatrum Botanicum* (1640), the name *"Yucca"* from *Yuca* had become too well established and has remained unchanged to this day. The threads on the leaf margins account for *filamentosa*, from the Latin *filum*, "thread."

HERBS

BALM
(lemon balm, sweet balm)
Melissa officinalis L.
Mint family
(Lamiaceae [Labiatae])

A hardy perennial, 3–4 feet,
balm has nettle-shaped leaves
and small, 2–lipped whitish flowers. Blooming June–October, it
was native to southern Europe.

Balm closed wounds without danger of infection. The dried
leaves were used for nervous troubles, comforted the heart, and
dispelled melancholy. A sprig or two flavored wine cups. Balm
was a principal ingredient of *Eaux des Carmes,* which was distilled by Carmelite monks in seventeenth-century Paris and was
the forerunner of *Eau de Cologne.*

Lemon balm is a great bee-plant. Pliny observed that balm
helped strayed bees find their way home again. Centuries later,
Elizabethan beekeepers rubbed their beehives with balm leaves
because it "causeth the Bees to keepe together, and causeth
others to come unto them."

Melissa, from the Greek *Melis-
sophyllon,* "beloved by bees."

BURNET, SALAD
Sanguisorba minor Scop.
Rose family (Rosaceae)

Salad burnet is a perennial
herb native to Britain and Europe. Slender and branching

annual stems, 1–3 feet, spring erect from a basal rosette of leaves; the flowers, June–August, are gathered in a purplish head.

Francis Bacon, the Elizabethan statesman-writer, recommended making paths of the herb "for the perfume yielded by being trodden on and crushed." Salad burnet was formerly grown, however, as a salad herb and to flavor cool drinks, the young leaves having the quality of freshly cut cucumber.

Sanguisorba, from *sanguis*, "blood," *sorbere*, "soaking up," alludes to the medicinal use in stanching or checking blood.

CORIANDER

Coriandrum sativum L.
Carrot family
(Apiaceae [Umbelliferae])

Coriander is an annual herb that grows 1–2 feet. Its bright green foliage is like that of parsley but is more jagged, the delicate umbels of pale mauve flowers opening July–August. Charlemagne ordered coriander to be grown on the imperial farms. The aromatic seeds were used as a stimulant and a spice; today the seeds are used as an ingredient in curry powder and as a flavoring in liquors.

Coriandrum, from the Greek *koros*, "a bug," for the fetid smell of the leaves; the Latin *sativus* means "planted for crops."

DANDELION, COMMON

Taraxacum officinale Weber
Aster family
(Asteraceae [Compositae])

Common dandelion, with its many flowered yellow heads

up to 2 inches across, is perhaps the most familiar European weed in North America. Were it not so invasive, dandelion would be regarded as an exotic. Every part—flower, leaf, and roots—is useful. Of considerable medicinal value, young dandelion roots were long gathered from European meadows. Eventually the plant was "improved" and was grown for greens which, when blanched, were used for salad. It became an important item in the Central Market of Paris.

There are many species of dandelion. In the 1880s Japanese florists developed a species closely related to *T. officinale;* some 24 varieties in white, orange, black, and copper shades were grown, and in the early 1900s Japan had a dandelion society.

Dandelion has been known by about 50 common names; the oldest was the medieval Latin *dens leonis,* "lion's tooth"—from which came the French *dent-de-lion,* hence "dandelion." *Taraxacum* was derived through Latin and Arabic from the Persian *talkh chakok,* "bitter herb."

ELECAMPANE
Inula helenium L.
Aster family
(Asteraceae [Compositae])

Elecampane is a striking perennial with huge downy leaves and clusters of shaggy bright yellow flowers that look somewhat like double sunflowers. It grows up to 4–5 feet in July and August.

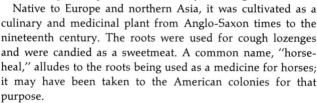

Native to Europe and northern Asia, it was cultivated as a culinary and medicinal plant from Anglo-Saxon times to the nineteenth century. The roots were used for cough lozenges and were candied as a sweetmeat. A common name, "horseheal," alludes to the roots being used as a medicine for horses; it may have been taken to the American colonies for that purpose.

In Italy the plant grew wild on the Campania and "Elecampane" is a corruption of *Enula campane.* In mythology, Helen of Troy is said to have had her hands full of the plant when Paris carried her away to Phrygia— hence *Inula helenium.*

FENNEL

Foeniculum vulgare Mill
(syn. *F. officinale* All.)
Carrot family
(Apiaceae [Umbelliferae])

Fennel is a graceful 4–6-foot ornamental with feathery leaves and bright golden flowers in flattopped umbels.

The Romans cultivated the plant for the aromatic seeds and the succulent edible shoots; nibbled on fast days, the licorice-flavor seeds satisfied hunger cravings. Edward I's household account records that $8\frac{1}{2}$ pounds of fennel seed were purchased as one month's supply. In *Acetaria, A Discourse of Sallets* (1693), Evelyn asserted that the soft white peeled stalks, when dressed like celery, invited sleep. The leaves were used for garnishing and flavoring fish dishes, and as an ingredient of "gripe water" given to babies with indigestion. The Italians have taken fennel with them wherever they have made a home away from home, and fennel now grows wild in many parts of the world.

Foeniculum was the Romans' name and was derived from the Latin *foenum,* a fragrant variety of hay.

FEVERFEW

Chrysanthemum parthenium (L.) Bernh.
Aster family
(Asteraceae [Compositae])

Native to Europe and probably to Britain, feverfew is a perennial that grows to 2½ feet and has chrysanthemumlike, bitter tasting leaves. Numerous small white-rayed flowers with yellow centers bloom June–August.

A cold infusion of the flowers was taken as a general tonic; a tincture of the plant, applied instantly, relieved the pain and swelling caused by insect bites. Feverfew was taken to allay fevers and was planted around dwellings to purify the atmosphere and to ward off disease. The name feverfew is a corruption of *febrifuge.* The plant was also called featherfew or featherfoil.

Chrysanthemum means "golden flower"; *parthenium* because the plant reputedly saved the life of a man who fell from a height and became "giddie in the head" during the building of the Parthenon.

HORSERADISH

Armoracia rusticana Meyer,
Gaert. & Schreb.
(syn. *Cochlearia armoracia* L.)
Mustard family
(Brassicaceae [Cruciferae])

Found in many parts of Europe, horseradish's origin is obscure. A hardy perennial, it has large oblong leaves with serrated edges and inconspicuous flowers.

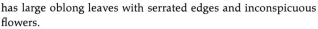

Both roots and leaves were used medicinally in the Middle Ages. The inner root, snow white when freshly grated, was used as a digestive stimulant. In England in the 1600s, the grated root was also used as a condiment with fish; later, the root provided the hot and biting horseradish sauce traditionally eaten with roast beef.

Cochleare from the name of an old-fashioned spoon, the leaves of many species being shaped like the bowl of a spoon; *armoracia* was the old Latin name for the plant.

LAVENDER

Lavandula angustifolia Mill.
(syn. *L. spica* L.;
L. officinalis Chaix)
Mint family (Lamiaceae [Labiatae])

Upward of 25 species of lavender are found from the Canary
Islands to India; several are
native to the Mediterranean region. *L. angustifolia,* often described as Old English lavender, is a shrub, to 3 feet, with gray
leaves and whorls of fragrant pale blue (lavender) flowers
clustering at the top of stiff, straight stems or spikes.

For centuries it has been customary to dry the spikes for the
sweet clean fragrance of the flowers, which Parkinson described
as "piercing the senses." Dried lavender was used to scent
linen; oil of lavender was extracted for making lavender water.

Lavandula from the Latin *lavo,* "to wash," alluding to the
preparation of lavender water.

THE MARJORAMS

Origanum
Mint family (Lamiaceae [Labiatae])

Marjorams are warmly aromatic herbs. The two kinds included
here have been subject to confusion and changes of name.
Origanum, probably first applied to *O. vulgare,* is from the Greek
oros, "mountain"; *ganos,* joy—"joy of the mountain," is for the
gay appearance that the plant gives to the hillsides on which it
grows when it is in flower.

Majorana (sweet marjoram) is from the Arabic *marjamie.*

WILD MARJORAM

(common marjoram, oregano)
Origanum vulgare L.

Before 1940 common marjo-
ram was called wild marjoram
in American cookbooks. In the
United States today it is known as oregano; in France it is
origan. A perennial, 2–4 feet, it has reddish stalks and purplish
2–lipped flowers in June and July. Native to Britain and Europe,
wild marjoram was esteemed as a medicinal herb, while the
cultivated kinds were more commonly used for culinary purposes. The fresh flowering tops were used, however, to flavor
ale, and the fresh or dried leaves, to flavor soups and stews. It
was valued as a bee-plant. A tea of dried leaves was reputed to
be a remedy for narcotic poison and convulsions and the essential oil was useful for toothache. The flowering tops also
yielded a reddish brown dye.

SWEET MARJORAM

(knotted or garden marjoram)
Majorana hortensis Moench
(syn. *Origanum majorana* L.)

Sweet marjoram is a low,
tender, bushy perennial, 12–18
inches, from northern Africa.
The whitish purplish flowers, in June, are almost hidden in the
knotlike clusters of tiny leaves growing close together at the
tops of the stems—hence the name "knotted." The herb was
known as "Margeron gentle," being sweeter and more delicate

in flavor than the larger, coarser wild plant. Izaak Walton in *The Compleat Angler* (1653) recommended its use with freshly caught fish; today it is one of the 12 most-used herbs in French cooking. Parkinson said that sweet marjoram was used "to please the outward senses in nosegays and in the windows of houses. . . ." Until late in the eighteenth century the herb was "raised in the flower garden for the sake of nosegays."

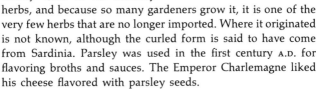

PARSLEY

Petroselinum crispum (Mill.)
S. W. Hill (syn. *P. hortense*)
Carrot family
(Apiaceae [Umbelliferae])

Parsley is too well known to need description. It is the most widely used of all culinary herbs, and because so many gardeners grow it, it is one of the very few herbs that are no longer imported. Where it originated is not known, although the curled form is said to have come from Sardinia. Parsley was used in the first century A.D. for flavoring broths and sauces. The Emperor Charlemagne liked his cheese flavored with parsley seeds.

Petroselinum, from the Greek *petros*, a stone—a plant often found growing among seacoast rocks.

ROSEMARY

Rosmarinus officinalis L.
Mint family
(Lamiaceae [Labiatae])

Rosemary, from the Mediterranean region, is an evergreen shrub that grows 2–6 feet. The

leaves, like curved pine needles, are deep green, silver under-
neath, and yield a pungent fragrance when rubbed. The flowers
are small, pale blue, and often open early in the year in warm
climates.

The herb was variously used: as a condiment for salted
meats, for rosemary tea, to flavor ale and wine, as a fragrant
moth repellent, to substitute for costly incense, and for decking
churches at festivals, such as Christmastime. Greek students
twined rosemary in their hair when studying, believing it an aid
to memory. Sir Thomas More grew the herb because his bees
loved it, and because "it is the herb sacred to remembrance and
therefore to friendship."

Rosmari-nus, from the Latin for
"sea-dew," because the plant
was supposed to grow best
within the sound of the sea.

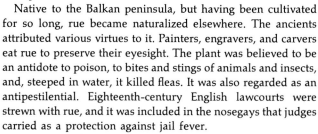

RUE

Ruta graveolens L.
Rue family (Rutaceae)

Rue, an evergreen rounded
plant, 2–3 feet tall, has finely
cut, acrid smelling, gray green
foliage and panicles of soft greenish yellow flowers from June
to September.

Native to the Balkan peninsula, but having been cultivated
for so long, rue became naturalized elsewhere. The ancients
attributed various virtues to it. Painters, engravers, and carvers
eat rue to preserve their eyesight. The plant was believed to be
an antidote to poison, to bites and stings of animals and insects,
and, steeped in water, it killed fleas. It was also regarded as an
antipestilential. Eighteenth-century English lawcourts were
strewn with rue, and it was included in the nosegays that judges
carried as a protection against jail fever.

Rue was also known as Herb of Grace. The origin of its name
is obscure, although *ruta,* the old Latin name from the Greek
rhyte, "to preserve," also means repentance.

THE SAGES

Salvia

Mint family (Lamiaceae [Labiatae])

There are more than 700 species of sage; perennial herbs, sub-shrubs, and shrubs distributed widely in both hemispheres. Sage comes from *saluge*, the old English translation of *salvia*. *Salvia*, the Latin name used by Pliny derived from *salveo*, "to save" or "heal," alludes to the medicinal qualities of some species.

CLARY SAGE

S. sclarea L.

One of the stateliest of the sages, this biennial has large, wrinkled, heart-shaped, stem-clasping leaves. The 2–lipped pinkish mauve flowers and big pink bracts, in whorls, are carried on 2–foot spires.

When soaked in water, the suds form a thick mucilage that is used to remove grit from eyes (clear eye is another common name), to draw out thorns, and to soothe inflammation. Clary oil was used as a fixative in perfumery and to flavor wines. It reached England from Europe in 1562.

COMMON SAGE

S. officinalis L.

Common or garden sage, which grows in stony places in southern Europe, has been cultivated for centuries for culinary and medicinal purposes. It is a small shrub, to 2 feet, with a woody stem and "sage green" velvety leaves. This species rarely flowers and is thus preferred by commercial growers.

Sage leaves are strongly and distinctively flavored, and a little goes a long way in seasoning. The Romans called it *herba sacra*, regarding it as a cure for cholera and for numerous other ills. Sage tea was valued as a health-giving drink, and at one time the Chinese imported sage from Holland at the rate of 3 pounds of China tea to 1 pound of the dried sage leaves.

SAVORY

Satureja
Mint family (Lamiaceae [Labiatae])

Summer and winter savory are highly aromatic herbs of the Mediterranean region. Before the use of East Indian spices, they were used for seasoning far more than they are today. Josselyn listed both. Savory means "pleasing to the taste." *Satureja* was the old Latin name used by Pliny, savory being the chosen plant of the satyrs.

SUMMER SAVORY

S. hortensis L.

Summer savory is an erect, slender annual, 6–12 inches, with blunt leaves and small purplish nearly white flowers that bloom in the axils of the leaves in July. This is the savory of commerce. Virgil counted it among the most fragrant herbs and recommended that it be grown near the beehives for rubbing on wasp and bee stings— for its fragrancy, not for its medicinal use.

WINTER SAVORY
S. montana L.

Winter savory is a woody perennial that grows as a little bush, to 1 foot, with small pointed leaves and small, almost white flowers in the axils of the leaves. More pungent than summer savory, it is mixed with other herbs to induce its hot spiciness. It has no medicinal value, but in Tudor times was used in making knot-gardens.

SPEARMINT
(common mint)
Mentha spicata L.
(syn. *M. viridis* L.)
Mint family
(Lamiaceae [Labiatae])

Spearmint is a perennial, to 2 feet; tapering spikes of purplish lilac flowers in whorls in the axils of the upper leaves bloom July–August. This is the mint most commonly grown for culinary purposes—to flavor sauces and to prevent milk from curdling.

The Romans used mint, like balm, in baths as a restorative to comfort and strengthen the sinews. One English herbalist named nearly 40 maladies for which mint is "singularly good." The plant, native to the Mediterranean region, is so old in cultivation that its exact origin is unknown. Elder William Brewster grew it in Plymouth, Massachusetts, in the early 1600s; Josselyn also noted it.

Some say that the old Latin name *Mentha* is from the Greek name of Minthe, the nymph whom Persephone changed into an aromatic plant. The name is, however, considered to stem from an older, vanished language spoken in the Mediterranean region 3,000–4,000 years ago. *Spicata,* "spiked," describes the spikelike flower stalks.

STRAWBERRY

(scarlet or Virginia strawberry)
Fragaria virginiana Duchesne
Rose family (Rosaceae)

On April 28, 1608, the Virginia colonists, having entered Chesapeake Bay, landed and explored near Point Comfort. Wrote George Percy: "We past through excellent ground . . . Going a little further we came into a little plat of ground full of fine and beautiful Strawberries, foure times bigger and better than ours in England." Five days after the landing at Jamestown, Percy again noted the "many strawberries growing in the woods."

Parkinson included "the Virginia Strawberry" in his *Paradisus* (1629). Other established favorites were the native wood strawberry and the European alpine and hautboy strawberries. Just over 100 years after the founding of Jamestown, a French army officer sent to spy on the Spanish colonies of Chile and Peru took back to France some strawberry plants from Chile's coastal regions. When propagated, the Chile plant was sent to Holland, and from there to Miller in England (1729). *F. chiloensis* Duchesne bore purplish red berries, even larger than *F. virginiana.* In either France or Holland a chance cross occurred between the two plants, and the resulting hybrid was named the pineapple strawberry (*F. chiloensis ananassa* var. Bailey), its scent, shape, and taste resembling that of the pineapple. Not until 1766, however, did Antoine Nicolas Duchesne, the French botanist, identify the parentage of the new fruit. The pineapple strawberry and its hybrids have given us the strawberries we enjoy today.

Before the discovery of either the Virginia or the Chile strawberry, English physicians and apothecaries believed the fruit to be of medicinal value. In the 1500s it was both an ornament and a table delicacy. In 1766 Duchesne observed that the English cultivated the long-stemmed *hautbois,* or hautboy strawberry, "to adorn their tables."

Several suggestions have been given for the origin of the

word "strawberry." The name may be derived from the Anglo-Saxon *streow*, "hay"; for the "hayberry" ripening at haymaking time; or from the children's custom of selling the berries strung on straw or dried grass. Or the name may have been used to describe the way the runners *strew* or strayed away from the mother plant to find space in which to grow. *Fragaria* comes from *fraga*, the old Latin name derived from *fragrans*, "fragrant," in reference to the fruit.

TANSY

Tanacetum vulgare L.
(syn. *Chrysanthemum vulgare* [L.] Bernh.)

Tansy, a native to Britain and Europe, is a perennial herb, to 3–5 feet, with broad, deeply divided feathery leaves and angled stems branching off into flat clusters of yellow flower heads in August and September.

The leaves have a camphorlike scent and were scattered over the floor of a room to keep it free of fleas and flies. Tansy tea was used as a stimulant and tonic and to treat fevers and various nervous ailments; and tansy was an ingredient in many colonial and nineteenth-century recipes.

Tanacetum is from the Latin *tanazeta*, the eastern European name.

THYME

Thymus vulgaris L.
Mint family
(Lamiaceae [Labiatae])

Common or garden thyme, native to southern Europe, is

a small, spreading aromatic bush, 6–8 inches, evergreen, with a mass of tiny lavender flowers from June to August.

The herb was probably grown in England long before the given date of 1548—Gerard considered it so common as to need no description. A favorite bee-plant, it was frequently planted near the hives, and there was an old belief that the abundance of its flowering foretold the year's honey yield. It was also a strewing herb and was used medicinally and as a flavoring. Paths were made of the "creeping" varieties.

Thymus was the Greek name used by Theophrastus, probably for another species. It may have come from a word meaning "to fumigate," because thyme was used as an incense to perfume and purify temples.

WORMWOOD

Artemisia absinthium L.
Aster family
(Asteraceae [Compositae])

Common wormwood, a bitter herb native to Britain and Europe, is a herbaceous perennial, to 3 feet, with finely cut silvery foliage and panicles of small yellow flowers in late July.

A strewing herb, the dried tops and leaves were also placed among clothes to repel moths. Josselyn listed it.

"Wormwood" is so named because its essential oil is a worm-expeller. *Artemisia* is from the Greek Artemis, who is identified with the goddess Diana of Roman mythology. *Absinthium* was the old generic name; absinthal, when extracted from wormwood, is the basis of absinth, the liqueur.

Biographical Appendix

The following biographical notes concern only those plantsmen whose names have occurred in the preceding pages. There were countless others. Many belonged to one or more of three influential groups—the Royal Society, the Company of Gardeners, and the Society of Gardeners briefly described at the outset.

THE ROYAL SOCIETY (more fully, the Royal Society of London for Improving Natural Knowledge) is usually considered to have been founded in 1660. A nucleus had been formed some years earlier, however, by "divers worthy persons, inquisitive into natural philosophy and other parts of human learning, and particularly of what hath been called the *New Philosophy* or *Experimental Philosophy.*" The charter of incorporation was granted in 1662.

From its founding the society encouraged collectors in North America, and correspondence with continental philosophers and naturalists was an important part of the society's work. Selections from this correspondence, describing some of the "present undertakings, studies and labours of the Ingenious in many considerable parts of the world," were published in the society's highly important *Philosophical Transactions.* Much of the information was received from Mark Catesby, John Mitchell, and Alexander Garden.

The Royal Society burgeoned into an exclusive club whose membership included eminent men in Britain and in the North American colonies. Exclusiveness did not rest merely on birth and fortune; talent and ability were carefully weighed. The names of fellows of the Royal Society, men concerned with the miracles of nature in new lands overseas, were well known in those households that shared the same interest.

THE COMPANY OF GARDENERS of London was commonly called the Worshipful Company of Gardeners. From early times the practitioners of various trades and crafts in the City of London formed themselves into guilds, each exercising a monopoly in its own field. The first record of a guild of gardeners is in 1345. The guild was incorporated into a company by charter of James I in 1606. One of the reasons for setting up the Company of Gardeners was to maintain the high quality of produce sold to the public; another was to prohibit anyone from exercising "the Art or Mystery of Gardening" within six miles of the City of London without the "Consent of the Company." The company also laid down where produce was to be sold, and, to keep the City clean, had "the dung and noysommes of the citie" taken away. It employed "thousands of poore people, ould men, women and children, in sellings of their Commodities, in weedinge, in gatherings of Stone, Etc., which would be otherwise veerie burdensome to the cittie, and suburbes thereof."

THE SOCIETY OF GARDENERS. Mention should be made of the Society of Gardeners, founded in the early 1700s, because it was essentially a gardener-nurseryman's society. Its members met once a month for five or six years at Newhall's Coffeehouse in Chelsea to discuss, register, and describe plants growing in their gardens. Under their influence floriculture was greatly advanced. Fairchild, Furber, and Miller were the leading members.

Three writers of classical antiquity, referred to repeatedly in today's botanical manuals and gardening dictionaries, head the list of short biographies. They are placed first, out of alphabetical order, because they are separated so far in time from the plantsmen and writers of colonial days.

THEOPHRASTUS (ca. 370 B.C.–ca. 286 B.C.), pupil and friend of Plato and Aristotle, author of *Enquiry into Plants* and many other books.

DIOSCORIDES (1st cent. A.D.), Greek physician whose *De Materia Medica*, on the names and healing virtues of the herbs known to him, remained the "bible" of all physicians throughout the Middle Ages.

PLINY the Elder (23–79 A.D.), an extraordinarily versatile Roman, a contemporary of Dioscorides. Pliny held many public offices, being at one time a governor of Iberia, and commander of the fleet. A voluminous writer, he dictated even while dressing after his bath. His *Natural History* runs to 37 volumes.

REVEREND JOHN BANISTER (1650–1692). English chaplain and naturalist sent to Virginia by Bishop Compton in 1678 in the role of clergyman as well as plant collector and naturalist. Banister introduced a number of plants into England, sending seeds to Bishop Compton and several other correspondents. His *Catalogue of Virginia Plants,* the first known work of its kind, was published in Ray's *Historia Planatarum,* vol. 2 (1688). Many descriptions and drawings in his unfinished writings were used in the works of his contemporaries. In his history, Beverley borrowed heavily from Banister's notes for a natural history of Virginia, reproducing whole passages almost verbatim. Shortly before his death, Banister took part in planning the establishment of the College of William and Mary. The Banister River near the Virginia–North Carolina border is named for him, as is a silvery leaved Brazilian climbing vine, *Banisteria argyrophylla.*

BENJAMIN SMITH BARTON (1766–1815). Pennsylvania-born, a professor of natural history and botany at the University of Pennsylvania who also became physician to the Pennsylvania Hospital. His *Elements of Botany* (1803) was the earliest botanical textbook published in the United States; some of its illustrations were derived from William Bartram's drawings. The book helped such botanical explorers as Thomas Nuttall, whom Barton trained as a collecting botanist, and Meriwether Lewis, who came to Barton for instruction in natural history before setting out with William Clark on the first transcontinental journey, 1804–1806.

JOHN BARTRAM (1699–1777). A Pennsylvania farmer of English Quaker descent who became America's first native botanist and, in Linnaeus's opinion, the greatest natural botanist of his day. By his late twenties Bartram had acquired a reputation for good farming. His home on the Schuylkill River, some 3 miles from Philadelphia, was of stone, quarried and built by his own hands. He stocked the nursery, laid out on 6 riverside acres, over the years with the plants he collected on his travels and received from correspondents overseas. It was one of the first plant collections in America, known informally as "Kingsess Botanical Garden." Officially, it bore the name John Bartram and Sons and, on Bartram's death in 1777, was carried on by his son, John Bartram, Jr., until the latter died in 1812.

Bartram was one of the first to experiment in hybridization. In quest of plants, he explored on foot and horseback and by boat thousands of miles from Canada to Florida. On one of his journeys through Virginia he visited Clayton, Byrd, and John Randolph, and spent two nights with Custis, who found him "the most taking facetious man I have ever met with, and never was so much delighted with a stranger in all my life."

Bartram had numerous correspondents on both sides of the Atlantic. He exchanged plants and seeds and corresponded with Collinson in London for nearly 40 years, from 1730 until Collinson's death in 1768. Through Collinson's influence he was appointed king's botanist by George III. Of the 300 new North American plants introduced into England between 1735 and 1780, Bartram and Collinson get credit for about two-thirds.

WILLIAM BARTRAM (1739–1823). Naturalist and artist, fifth son of John Bartram, whom he accompanied on some explorations. William was commissioned by Fothergill and the Duchess of Portland to draw a series of pictures of flowers and shells. These are among the most beautiful and imaginative of early North American illustrations. Fothergill also financed William's expedition to the South (1773–1778). His account, *Travels through North and South Carolina, Georgia, East and West Florida* (1791), with its vivid descriptions of plants and scenery, influenced the English romantic poets, Wordsworth and Coleridge.

ROBERT BEVERLEY (ca. 1673–1722). Son of a Virginia planter, Beverley was schooled in England, inherited a plantation from his father, and later acquired, from his half-brothers, an estate of 6,000 acres, named Beverley Park, in King and Queen County. He married the sister of William Byrd II. She died in less than a year at the birth of a son, and Beverley never remarried. For a while he made Jamestown his home, to be nearer the seat of government, and represented Jamestown in the House of Burgesses. In 1703 Beverley went to England to prosecute an appeal to the Privy Council concerning some newly acquired houses and land. He stayed 18 months but lost his suit, which, along with his outspoken criticism of policies and people, damaged him financially and politically. Having no chance of political advancement, he withdrew to Beverley Park to live in an austere and simple style. He was proud of being a Virginian and, unlike other plantation owners who imported their furnishings from England, his furniture was made on the estate. Beverley is remembered for his *History and Present State of Virginia* (1705), which ranks him as one of Virginia's first historians.

WILLIAM BYRD II (1674–1744). Like his father prominent in Virginia affairs as the holder of many public offices, Byrd continued his father's activities as explorer, trader, merchant, landowner, and politician. He was educated in England, studied in the Middle Temple, was admitted to the bar, and was named a Fellow of the Royal Society at the age of 21. He was a friend of many prominent men. Westover, the elegant plantation house he built on the banks of the James River, was renowned for its hospitality: "My doors are open to all." Peter Collinson, writing to John Bartram, said: "I am told Colonel Byrd has the best garden in Virginia, and a pretty greenhouse well furnished with Orange trees. I knew him well in England, and he was reckoned a very polite, ingenious man." He read Greek, Latin, and Hebrew and had one of the largest libraries in the colonies, which numbered some 4,000 books including botanical texts. His love of nature and his interest in fruit growing and medicinal herbs is evident in his own writings—the *Secret Diary*, written in shorthand and not intended for publication, the *Natural History of Virginia*, and the *History of the Dividing Line*. Above all, Byrd was a servant of the crown: he was a member of the House of Burgesses and, for 34 years, he was a member of the governor's Council, becoming its president in the last year of his life.

MARK CATESBY (1682–1749). An English naturalist who came to Williamsburg in 1712—his sister had married Dr. William Cocke, secretary to the Virginia colony—and roved the Tidewater for 7 years. Custis, Clayton, Mitchell, and Byrd were among his friends. After a stay in England, he traveled in the southern colonies and visited the Bahamas (1722–1726). Back home he settled down, intent on writing and illustrating a natural history, and supported himself by working in Fairchild's nursery. Collinson lent him money without interest. Preferring to paint his plants "fresh and just gather'd," he worked from some of his on-the-spot sketches and received a continuing supply of plants through Clayton, Custis, Byrd, and other friends in America. He learned to engrave, and colored all but two of the prints himself; these he engraved from drawings made for him by his friend Georg Dionysius Ehret (1708–1770), the greatest botanical artist of his day. Catesby's *Natural History of the Carolinas, Florida and Bahama Islands* (vol. 1, 1731, vol. 2, 1743) took 20 years to complete. It was one of the outstanding works of its kind before the Revolution and includes many Virginia plants. Catesby sparked Collinson's interest in North American plants and introduced a number of them himself.

REVEREND JOHN CLAYTON (1657–1725). English clergyman who, like Banister, came to Virginia in the dual role of naturalist-observer and clergyman. He was the minister of James City Parish (1684–1686), and, on his return to England, wrote several papers on his observations, some for the Royal Society.

JOHN CLAYTON (1694–1773). Son of the attorney general of the colony, he came to Virginia as a young man in about 1715. He is sometimes confused with the Reverend John Clayton, a distant kinsman. Clayton served as clerk of Gloucester County for 51 years and spent his leisure in studying and collecting plants. Linnaeus named the spring beauty *Claytonia virginica* for him. Clayton's correspondents were many and included John Frederick Gronovius (1690–1762), a physician-naturalist of Leyden, Holland. Clayton sent herbarium specimens to Gronovius and also his manuscript "Catalogue of Plants, Fruits and Trees Native to Virginia." Gronovius published *Flora Virginica* (part I in 1739, part II in 1743), generally accepted as the best systematic treatise of its period on American botany. Implied criticism has been made of Gronovius for publishing the book under his own name, thereby diminishing Clayton's part in it. Yet the title page gives a completely fair and honest statement: *Flora Virginica Exhibens Plantas Quas V. C.* [i.e., Vir Clarissimus] *Johannes Clayton In Virginia Observavit atque collegit. Easdem Methodo Sexuali disposuit, ad Genera propria retulit, Nominibus specificis insignivit, & minus cognitas descripsit Joh. Fred. Gronovius.* "Flora of Virginia: Presenting plants which the very distinguished man, John Clayton, observed and collected in Virginia. John Frederick Gronovius arranged these plants according to the sexual method, referred them to the proper genera, designated specific names for them, and described the poorly known ones." William T. Stearn, senior principal scientific officer, Department of Botany, of the British Museum's Division of Natural History, makes the authorship quite clear:

> Gronovius studied carefully the specimens sent to him by Clayton, most of which are in the British Museum (Natural History) mounted on the blank reverse side of cut-up pages of Linnaeus's *Systema Naturae* (1735), and he classified and named them according to Linnaeus's methods, which were, of course, unknown to Clayton out in Virginia. Throughout, although Clayton's names were unacceptable, Gronovius gave him full credit[;] but Gronovius, with Linnaeus's help, was undoubtedly the author of the *Flora Virginica*, not Clayton, and but for Gronovius's publication Clayton's work would lack modern relevance. *Journal of the Garden History Society*, III (summer 1975).

PETER COLLINSON (1694–1768). English Quaker and woolen merchant of London. "In the very early part of my life," Collinson recalled, "I had a love for gardening." He became a Fellow of the Royal Society when he was 35. His garden at Mill Hill near London was famous: "My Garden is now a Paradise of Delight," he wrote to Linnaeus in September 1765. Collinson imported seeds from all over the world, and John Bartram became his constant supplier of North American seeds and plants. In return Collinson sent him presents including books, a suit of clothes for Bartram, gowns for Mrs. Bartram, and gifts for their children.

Eventually, Bartram suggested he could give more time to collecting if he were regularly compensated. Certain influential

Englishmen agreed to pay small amounts per year to support Bartram's plant-hunting expeditions. On Bartram's behalf, Collinson supplied boxes of seeds and plants to dukes and earls, and to such well-known gardeners as William Penn and Philip Miller of the Chelsea Physic Garden. Collinson kept the accounts, purchased goods requested by Bartram, and sometimes sent him cash to settle the accounts, which he did annually. He sent Bartram £ 10 in halfpence on at least one occasion.

Bartram's seeds, in extraordinary quantities, went not only to English gardens but to the reforestation of estates in England, Scotland, Ireland, and eventually to Holland, France, and Germany. It is said that what Collinson and his North America coterie of correspondents did for both English and American gardens has no parallel elsewhere at any other time in garden history.

HENRY COMPTON (1632–1713). Bishop of London, head of the Anglican church in the American colonies, and first chancellor of the College of William and Mary in Virginia. His garden was one of England's finest. He was one of the first to encourage the importing of foreign plants and, according to Collinson, had a remarkable collection of American trees. At Fulham Palace, where he lived for 38 years, he had the advantage of watching his collection grow. He is also reputed to have had over 1,000 species of exotics under glass.

JOHN CUSTIS (1678–1749). John Custis of Williamsburg, as he is generally known, was educated in England, was a planter, a member of the House of Burgesses, and served on the Council for 22 years. He was among those correspondents Collinson called his "Brothers of the Spade." The two men exchanged plants and corresponded with one another for 12 years, from 1734 to 1746. In his day, Custis imported more European plants into the Tidewater than anyone else. John Bartram judged his garden as second only to Clayton's, and Collinson considered his collection of lilacs the best in America. He was William Byrd II's brother-in-law, and Washington married his son's widow, Martha.

JOHN EVELYN (1620–1706). English diarist and a founding member of the Royal Society. His *Kalendiarium Hortense* (1664) was the first published gardener's calendar. *Silva, or A Discourse of Forest-Trees* (1662) was prompted by Evelyn's concern for the wretched condition of English woodlands and forests. The *Silva* went into four editions in his lifetime; four more editions were printed between 1786 and 1815. *Acetaria, A Discourse on Sallets* appeared in 1693. Parkinson defined sallets as "many herbs growing wild in the fields, or else be but weeds in a Garden."

THOMAS FAIRCHILD (1667–1729). Gardener (nurseryman), clothworker of London, member of the Company of Gardeners and the Society of Gardeners. One of the first to experiment in hybridization and to concern himself with urban gardeners. His *City Gardener* (1722) dealt with the cultivation of plants that "thrive best in the London Gardens." He was one of the first if not the first to raise and distribute the tulip tree in quantity. Fairchild bequeathed a sum of money to be invested, the interest to provide for the preaching of a sermon each year on Tuesday in Whitsun week in St. Leonard's, Shoreditch, on "The Wonderful Works of God in the Creation" or "The certainty of the Resurrection of the Dead proved by the certain changes of the animal and vegetable parts of the Creation." The Fairchild Lecture is to this day delivered annually, the lecturer being appointed by the bishop of London.

JOHN FOTHERGILL (1712–1780). A London physician, a Quaker, and a member of the Society of Gardeners, who, under Collinson's guidance, laid out one of the finest gardens in England, which contained a collection of some 3,000 plants from all over the world. At Collinson's death, he became John Bartram's chief English correspondent and was also a patron of William Bartram.

ROBERT FURBER (ca. 1674–1756). A nurseryman and devout churchman, Furber served one term as overseer of the poor for the parish of St. Mary Abbot's, Kensington, and two terms as churchwarden. His catalogues of English and foreign trees and of the choicest fruit trees appeared together as one pamphlet in 1727, the earliest known nurseryman's catalogue issued as a pamphlet. In the preface Furber speaks of his career as a gardener: "This delightful employment I have for many years pursued, and have with all the skill and judgment I was master of, been collecting, propagating and improving great variety of the most curious and valuable trees, plants, fruit-trees, etc, both foreign and domestic." Furber's nursery in Kensington was, Collinson said, one of the most extensive in the first half of the eighteenth century. He bought many plants from the Fulham Palace garden after Bishop Compton's death. Furber was the first Englishman to publish a lavishly illustrated catalogue, *Twelve Months of Flowers* (1730). It contained 12 large hand-colored engravings, each showing the plants in bloom in one month of the year. A second edition in 1732 included a text and a new title, *The Flower-Garden Display'd*. The catalogue included 25 American plants, among them "the Virginian Aster" (*A. longifolium*) introduced by Catesby.

ALEXANDER GARDEN (1730–1791). A Scotsman, trained in medicine at Edinburgh, the 23-year-old doctor arrived in Charleston, South Carolina, in 1752. Garden was a plant collector with an ardent interest in taxonomy, and a significant member of the plant exchange group contributing to the science of classification of animals and plants. He practiced medicine at Charleston until 1782 and was regarded as its most able and beloved physician. He was, nonetheless, a loyalist, and was forced to remove to London, where he became a Fellow of the Royal Society. Linnaeus named the genus Gardenia for him.

JOHN GERARD (1545–1612). Born at Nantwich in Cheshire, Gerard practiced as a barber-surgeon in London. A skillful gardener, he also had charge of the gardens of Lord Burleigh, Queen Elizabeth's treasurer, and had a garden of his own at Holborn. There he assembled a remarkable collection of plants. His *Catalogus* printed in 1596 (*Catalogus arborum, fruticum ac planatarum tam indigernarum, quam exoticun, in horto Johannis ciuis*, revised and amplified in 1599) listed over 900 different kinds of plants that he grew at Holborn and was the first adequate record of its kind. The *Catalogus* included the first mention of many foreign plants, some of which may have been growing in English gardens for many years. Some Gerard noted as recent introductions. It later proved more useful than his *Herball* or *Historie of Plants* (1597). Thomas Johnson, a herbalist, brought out a corrected and enlarged edition of the *Herball* in 1633; it was one of the first botanical books in English rather than Latin.

THOMAS HARIOT or HARRIOT (1560–1621). English mathematician, surveyor, and astronomer; tutor to Walter Raleigh, who appointed him geographer on the second expedition to Virginia in 1588. Hariot's *A Brief and True Report of the New Found Land of Virginia* (1588), on its inhabitants and commodities, contains the first descriptions by an Englishman of many Virginia plants.

JOHN HILL (1716–1775). Hill tried his hand at many things, and for a time was a practicing apothecary. A prolific writer, his lavishly illustrated *The Vegetable Kingdom* in 25 volumes won him the king of Sweden's award, the Order of the Vase. Thereafter he styled himself Sir John Hill. Linnaeus wept at the sight of "such a costly work without botanical science." "Sir" John is chiefly remembered for *The British Herbal* (1756) and *Eden* (1757).

THOMAS JEFFERSON (1743–1826), third president of the United States. Jefferson spent much of his time between 1759 and 1770 at Williamsburg, first as a student at the College of William and Mary, then studying law under George Wythe, and later practicing in the General Court. As governor of Virginia (June 1779–June 1781) he resided in the Governor's Palace until the capital was removed to Richmond in 1780. Despite his range of activities (he was the president of the American Philosophical Society for 18 years, and the founder of the University of Virginia), Jefferson kept a "Farm Book" and a "Garden Book." The notes in the latter covered a span of 58 years (1766–1824). Inevitably there were gaps in the book when he was away from Monticello, the longest when he served as minister to France, (1784–1789). The Garden Book and his *Notes on the State of Virginia* (1784) are invaluable sources for the plants, including fruits and vegetables, cultivated at that period. The author of the Declaration of Independence counted among his important services the introductions of the olive tree and dry rice into South Carolina. In a letter to Charles Willson Peale in August 1811, Jefferson wrote:

I have often thought that if Heaven had given me choice of

my position and calling, it should have been a rich spot of earth, well watered, and near a good market for the productions of the garden. No occupation is so delightful to me as the culture of the earth, and no culture comparable to that of the garden. Such a variety of subjects, some one always coming to perfection, the failure of one thing repaired by the success of another, and instead of one harvest a continued one through the year. Under a total want of demand, except for our family table, I am still devoted to the garden. But though an old man, I am but a young gardener.

JOHN JOSSELYN (fl. 1630–1675). English naturalist who wrote on the plants and animals of New England, where he lived 1638–1639 and 1663–1671. His best known work is *New England Rarities Discovered* (1672).

PETER or PER KALM (1715–1779). Son of a poor Finnish pastor who became a botanist and professor of economy at the University of Åbo (now Turku). The Swedish Academy and three universities raised funds for Kalm to visit England and America to observe plants of economic value growing in a latitude similar to that of Sweden. He spent 6 months in England and over 2 years in America, collecting in the region between Philadelphia and Montreal. On his return home, Kalm was impoverished by his journeys and could only afford to publish his account at intervals. The first three volumes of *En Resa til Norra America* appeared in 1753, 1756, and 1761. The fourth and last part, although complete, was not in print at the time of his death, and the manuscript, still unpublished, was destroyed by fire in 1827. A translation from the original Swedish with new material from Kalm's diary notes appeared in 1770 under the title *Peter Kalm's Travels in North America*. Kalm's *Visit to England on his Way to America in 1748* was not published in London until 1892.

JOHN LAWSON (d. 1711). Englishman Lawson's urge for travel led him to New York. On being told "Carolina was the best country" for exploration, he set off for Charleston. He became surveyor-general of North Carolina. His *A New Voyage to Carolina: Containing the Exact Description and Natural History of that Country . . . And a Journal of a Thousand Miles, Travel'd Thro' several Nations of Indians* was printed in London in 1709.

CHARLES DE L'ECLUSE or CLUSIUS (1526–1609). Brilliant, versatile, Flemish botanist who spoke 8 languages. His *Rariorum Planatarium Historia* (1601) laid the foundation for much of Linnaeus's work. L'Ecluse, when he was a professor at Leyden, laid out the botanic garden there, and he is regarded as the chief founder of Holland's bulb growing trade.

CAROLUS LINNAEUS or CARL VON LINNÉ (1707–1778). A Swede, born of humble Lutheran parents, who became the most eminent botanist of his day. He traveled widely, corresponded with botanists all over the world, explored in Lapland, and gained an extraordinary knowledge of natural history. In 1741 he became professor of botany at the University of Uppsala, where he remained until his death; in 1761 Linnaeus was raised to the nobility and took the name von Linné, following the style his father had adopted.

Linnaeus's fame chiefly rests on his work in developing a sexual system for classifying plants, and creating a new format for naming them. In the binomial system of nomenclature he established, every living creature was distinguished by two Latin names—a generic name followed by a specific or descriptive name. The system applied only to wild species of plants and not to hybrids or horticultural varieties. Linnaeus's classification brought a measure of simplicity to the long descriptive Latin titles given to plants before his time and created some order in the previous confusion of species and varieties. His *Species Planatarum* (1753) has been internationally accepted as the basis for modern botanical naming systems in general. Although with the development of science his system of classification has been amended and modified, many of the underlying principles remain.

MATTHIAS DE LOBEL or L'OBEL (1538–1616). Native of France who, for political reasons, settled in England from ca. 1598 until his death and became botanist and physician to James I. L'Obel was the first to recognize and describe more than 80 new species of native British plants, and was a link between English and Continental gardeners. His most famous book, written in collaboration with Pierre Pena, *Stirpium Adversaris Nova* (1570), was dedicated to Queen Elizabeth I. The genus *Lobelia* was named for him.

ANDRÉ MICHAUX (1746–1802). Widely traveled French botanist, sent by the French government to Persia (he introduced numerous eastern plants into the botanic gardens of France). Michaux came to North America in 1785. His 15-year-old son, François André (1770–1855), accompanied him. He established a nursery garden just north of Charleston, South Carolina, and from there made a series of botanical explorations from Florida to Hudson's Bay. His *Histoire des Chênes d'Amérique* (1801) was translated under the title *North American Sylva* (1817–1819). *Flora Boreali-Americana,* published after his death, is believed to have been completed by François with the help of one or more other botanists. It is generally accepted as among the first North American flora published.

PHILIP MILLER (1691–1771). Son of a London market-gardener with a florist's business of his own, Miller became curator of the Chelsea Physic Garden in 1722, a post he held for 48 years until he was pensioned off the year before his death. Under his direction, the garden became world famous, ranking in importance with the Jardin des Plantes in Paris and other European botanic gardens. Miller succeeded so well in raising and acclimatizing plant introductions from all over the world that he was acclaimed as a "prince of gardeners." In 1732 he collected seed of the cotton plant grown in the garden and sent it to the young American colony of Georgia. He published his *Gardener and Florists' Dictionary* in 1724; his *Gardener's Dictionary* (1731) was translated into Dutch, French, and German, went into 8 editions, the last in 1768, and was the standard work in England and the American colonies.

JOHN MITCHELL (1711–1768). A physician, naturalist, plant lover, and cartographer—one of the ablest scientific men of his time in North America. Born and raised on a small plantation in tidewater Virginia, Mitchell studied botany and medicine at the University of Edinburgh and later practiced medicine for 15 years in Urbanna, Virginia. In 1746 he and his wife sailed to England where he lived for the rest of his life. He was elected a Fellow of the Royal Society and counted many of its members among his friends, including Collinson and Catesby. Linnaeus named the partridge berry (*Mitchella repens*) for him.

Mitchell took a part in the procuring of plants for the original planting of Kew Gardens, but his fame rests on the map of North America that he made in 1750–1755. The map was used by American and British officers during the Revolution, by the United States and British peace negotiators at its end, and in establishing national and state boundary lines thereafter—most recently in 1932. His obituaries identified him as the man "who made the new map of North America." A copy of a late edition of the map hangs in the West Advance Building of the Governor's Palace in Williamsburg.

NICHOLAS MONARDES (ca. 1493–1588). A physician of Seville, Spain, author of a book on the resources of the West Indies, and the first to describe the flora of the Americas. The book, published in 1561, was translated into English in 1577 under the title *Joyful Newes out of the Newe Founde Worlde.* The tobacco plant was first described and illustrated in it.

THOMAS NUTTALL (1786–1859). A Yorkshire-born Englishman, a printer by trade but with a bent for natural history, who came to Philadelphia when he was 22 years old and was trained as a collecting botanist by Professor Barton. Member of the Academy of Sciences of Philadelphia, and curator of Harvard University's botanic garden (1822–1834), Nuttall was probably the most widely traveled plant collector of his time. His journeys led him to almost every state of the union, walking many thousands of miles on foot.

Nuttall's fame as a botanist rests chiefly on his *Genera of North American Plants;* as an ornithologist on his *Manual of Ornithology of the United States and Canada.* In *North American Sylva* he described some forest trees of the United States, Canada, and Nova Scotia not included in Michaux's *Sylva.* He set most of the type for his work himself. His friend Audubon named the western dogwood (*Cornus nuttallii*) for him.

JOHN PARKINSON (1567–1650). A London apothecary who became king's botanist to Charles I, and author of *Paradisi in Sole, Paradisus Terrestris* (1629). In his great book, Parkinson describes about a thousand plants—"their nature, place of birth, time of flowering, names and virtues of each plant, useful in physic, or admired for beauty." Up to that time plants had been recommended only for their usefulness; that they should be admired for their beauty was a new approach. Parkinson was the first to describe many of the plants that he listed, although some may have been growing in English gardens before 1629. *Theatrum Botanicum, A Herball of a Large Extent,* was printed in 1640.

JOSEPH PRENTIS (1754–1809). A judge of the General Court of Virginia and prominent in public affairs, Judge Prentis lived at Green Hill, a large property that probably formed the block bounded by Nassau, Scotland, Henry, and Prince George streets in Williamsburg. His father, William Prentis, lived in the house on Duke of Gloucester Street known today as the Prentis House. His "Garden Book" (March 1784–February 1788) and "Monthly Kalender" (1775–1779) have survived in manuscript at the University of Virginia, and are concerned chiefly with the growing of vegetables and herbs.

WILLIAM PRINCE (1766–1842) was the third proprietor of the Prince Nursery at Flushing, New York, if we name Robert Prince, his grandfather, as the founder of this family concern, although some biographical notices credit Robert's son William, Sr., as the founder sometime between 1737 and 1750. The Prince Nursery became a famed center of horticulture in America, the nursery's catalogues ranking among the standard reference publications over a considerable period. As far as is known, the first advertisement appeared in 1767, and the nursery continued until sometime in the 1860s with Robert William Prince as its fourth proprietor. In April 1781 Thomas Jefferson ordered a number of shrubs, shade trees, and fruit trees from the Prince Nursery, receiving them in November. When he was living at Matoax, Virginia, St. George Tucker enlarged his orchard in 1787 by planting 120 fruit trees that he "bought of William Prince on Long Island."

JOHN RANDOLPH (1727–1784). The last king's attorney under the crown for the Virginia colony, known as John the Tory, he was a loyalist who went "home" to England on the eve of the Revolution. Modeled on Philip Miller's *Gardener's Dictionary,* his *Treatise on Gardening,* the first kitchen garden calendar, was printed in America about 1788. Previously, only books written for gardening in the climate of England had been available.

JOHN RAY (1627–1705). Son of an English blacksmith, scholar of Trinity College, Cambridge, Anglican clergyman, naturalist, and plant collector in Europe and Britain. Ray received seeds from Banister and published Banister's catalogue of plants, which he had received from Bishop Compton after Banister's death, in volume 2 of his *Historia Plantarum* (1688). His *Methodus Planatarum Nova* (1682) was the basis of later English floras.

JOHN REA (d. 1681). Little is known about Rea. He is believed to have been a nurseryman, and in his *Flora, Ceres and Pomona* (1665) he tells us, "By long continued diligence, over forty years of allegiance to that lovely recreation I have collected all those rare plants, fruits, and flowers that by any means I could procure." He was one of the first commercial florists, and his son-in-law, Samuel Gilbert, author of the *Florist's Vade Mecum,* described him as "the best florist of his time."

LADY SKIPWITH (d. 1826). Jean and her husband, Sir Peyton Skipwith, lived at Prestwould on the Dan River, Virginia. An ardent gardener, her *Garden Notes* (1793) add to the records of flowers grown in the gardens of that time.

JOHN SMITH (1571–1631), usually distinguished as Captain John Smith. Orphaned at 16, but by no means penniless, the young Englishman was at heart an adventurer and became by profession a mercenary soldier. He alternately fought and traveled in Europe, Asia, and Africa. Sailing with the first band of Jamestown settlers, he explored and mapped the Chesapeake Bay and its inlets, creeks, and rivers as far as the fall line, and was named president of the Council in 1608. From 1610 to 1617 he explored in Canada and what was then known as "northern Virginia." At John Smith's request, Prince Charles (later Charles I) renamed this area New England.

Smith was the chief publicist for Virginia and for himself. His writings include *A True Relation of Virginia* (1608), *A Description of New England* (1616), and *The Generall Historie of Virginia, New-England and the Summer Isles* (1624). *True Travels* was printed the year before his death. His *Map of Virginia* (1612) of the bay and rivers also gave the location of nearly 200 Indian villages in the tidewater region. It is a most detailed and remarkably accurate map of Virginia made during the first 100 years of settlement. Some 27 adaptations and reproductions of the map were produced by seventeenth-century cartographers. It was cited as late as 1873 in the Maryland–Virginia boundary dispute.

WILLIAM STRACHEY (fl. 1600–1621). It is not definitely known whether the Strachey prominent in Virginia colonization was the elder or younger of the two men of that name, father and son, who flourished at the time. However this may be, the Strachey with whom history is concerned was an Englishman, a traveler, an author, and a scholar, who was among those accompanying Sir Thomas Gates, appointed by the London Company to act as Virginia's first governor. The *Sea Venture,* in which Gates and Strachey sailed, was wrecked at Bermuda Islands on July 25, 1609. In *A True Repertory of the Wracke* Strachey told how the party built another boat and reached Jamestown on May 23 of the following year. His account may have suggested to Shakespeare the setting of *The Tempest.* Strachey, appointed a member of the Council and recorder general of Virginia, returned to England after about a year's stay. His most important work was his *Historie of Travaile into Virginia Britannia,* written about 1618 and published by the Hakluyt Society in 1849.

JOHN TRADESCANT (d. 1638). Known as John Tradescant the Elder to distinguish him from his son John (1608–1662). Both were famous gardeners and plant collectors, and both in succession were appointed gardener to Charles I. Tradescant was appointed the royal gardener in 1629, the year that Parkinson published his *Paradisi.* He was, said Parkinson, a "painful industrious searcher and lover of all nature's varieties." He scoured Europe for plants, and accompanied Sir Dudley Digges on the latter's trade mission to Russia in 1618. Tradescant's notebook on the expedition contains the first known English list of Russian plants. He was a subscriber to the Virginia Company and a friend of Captain John Smith, who doubtless sent him plants and left Tradescant some of the books he carried in his sea chest. Tradescant's house at Lambeth, on the south side of the Thames, was known as the "Ark." In it he displayed an extraordinary collection of curiosities, "toyes" he and others brought from overseas. His garden was full of rare trees and plants. There were other good gardeners, but it was generally acknowledged that many of the "outlandish" or foreign plants "flow'red fully only with Mr. Tradescant." Among the plants he was the first to grow was the spiderwort named for him— *Tradescantia virginiana.*

JOHN TRADESCANT the Younger (1608–1662). Succeeded his father as gardener to Charles I. In 1634, then 26 years old, he was admitted as a freeman of the Company of Gardeners. In 1637 he came to Virginia, according to an entry in the state papers, "to gather all rarieties of flowers, plants, shells, etc." He returned to Virginia in 1642 and again in 1654 and on each occasion was granted a headright. In all, he was entitled to 100 acres somewhere in the Yorktown region for which he paid £ 500. It is fair to assume that he stayed with Edward Digges, fourth son of his father's friend, Sir Dudley Digges, at his plantation on the York River.

After the death of Charles I, Tradescant devoted himself to the Ark and its garden. In a catalogue of his collection, *Museum Tradescantianum* (1656), he added 30 to 40 more North American plants to the earlier list, among them the red maple, the tulip tree, and the coral honeysuckle.

ST. GEORGE TUCKER (1752–1827) is here remembered as a prominent citizen of Williamsburg who interested himself in growing fruit and nut trees. St. George Tucker was born in Port Royal, Bermuda. He enrolled at the College of William and Mary in 1771, studied law as a private student or clerk under George Wythe, and, in the spring of 1775, was admitted to practice before the General Court. He married the widow of John Randolph of Matoax, Virginia, and after her death in 1788 made Williamsburg his home. He accepted a seat on the General Court of Virginia and succeeded George Wythe as professor of law at the College. A number of his close-written pocket-sized almanacs, in which he recorded his orchard plantings, are now in the Tucker–Coleman Papers at the College of William and Mary.

WILLIAM TURNER (ca. 1510–1568). English botanist, ultimately dean of Wells Cathedral. Turner was the first to write a scientific botany and to attempt to identify and classify the British flora. He gave an English name to many native plants. *A New Herball,* previously issued in 3 separate parts, was printed in its entirety in Cologne in 1568.

THOMAS WALTER (ca. 1740–1788). An Englishman who, as a young man, settled on the Santee River in South Carolina. His *Flora Caroliniana* (1789), which lists more than 1,000 plants that he collected within an area of 25 square miles, is remarkably complete.

GEORGE WASHINGTON (1732–1799) first president of the United States. As a member of the House of Burgesses, Washington visited Williamsburg frequently and married Martha Dandridge, widow of Daniel Parke Custis, son of John Custis of Williamsburg. Beautifying the "pleasure grounds" at his plantation Mount Vernon was one of his chief recreations. The plan reflected his appreciation of the principles of contemporary European design. The grounds are among the outstanding examples of late eighteenth-century landscaping in America. He laid out a kitchen garden in 1766 and a flower garden several years later. Washington exchanged seeds and plants with his friends and correspondents and received many gifts of plants from his overseas admirers. André Michaux, the French botanist, visited Mount Vernon and brought seeds and plants. In 1792 Washington purchased a large number of ornamentals from John Bartram, Jr. The entries in his diary are brief: for example, January 19, 1785—"Employed until dinner in laying out my Serpentine road and shrubberries adjoining." He described his requirements for a gardener in 1788: "He is to be a compleat Kitchen Gardener with a complete knowledge of Flowers and a Green House." An entry in his Account Book, November 19, 1792, reads "By a large Watering Pot for the Garden 0.10.6."

Bibliography

Allan, Mea. *The Tradescants: Their Plants, Gardens and Museum, 1570–1662.* London: M. Joseph, 1964.

Andrews, A. W. *The Coming of the Flowers.* London: Williams & Norgate, 1950.

Ayres, Edward. "Fruit Culture in Colonial Virginia." 1973. Typescript in Department of Research, Colonial Williamsburg Foundation.

Bailey, L. H. *Manual of Cultivated Plants Most commonly grown in the continental United States and Canada.* Rev. ed. New York: The Macmillan Co., 1949.

―――. *Sketch of the Evolution of Our Native Fruits.* Reprint of 1898 ed. Wilmington, Del.: Scholarly Resources, 1974.

―――. *The Standard Cyclopedia of Horticulture.* 3 vols. New York: The Macmillan Co., 1925.

Berkeley, Edmund, and Berkeley, Dorothy Smith. *Dr. Alexander Garden of Charles Town.* Chapel Hill, N. C.: University of North Carolina Press, 1969.

―――. *Dr. John Mitchell: The Man Who Made the Map of North America.* Chapel Hill, N. C.: University of North Carolina Press, 1974.

―――. *John Clayton, Pioneer of American Botany.* Chapel Hill, N. C.: University of North Carolina Press, 1963.

Beverley, Robert. *The History and Present State of Virginia* (1705). Edited by Louis B. Wright. Chapel Hill, N. C.: University of North Carolina Press, 1947.

Blunt, Wilfred. *The Art of Botanical Illustration.* London: Collins, 1950.

Byrd, William. *Natural History of Virginia, or the Newly Discovered Eden.* Translated and edited from a German version by

Richmond Croom Beatty and William J. Mulloy. Richmond, Va.: Dietz Press, 1950.

————. *Histories of the Dividing Line betwixt Virginia and North Carolina.* Edited by William K. Boyd. Raleigh, N. C.: North Carolina Historical Commission, 1929.

Catesby, Mark. *The Natural History of Carolina, Florida and the Bahama Islands . . .* 2 vols. London: 1731, 1743.

Chittenden, Fred J., ed. *Royal Horticultural Society Dictionary of Gardening.* Reprinted from corrected sheets of the 2nd ed. London: Clarendon Press, 1965.

Coats, Alice M. *The Book of Flowers: Four Centuries of Flower Illustration.* New York: McGraw-Hill, 1973.

————. *Flowers and Their Histories.* London: A. & C. Black, 1968.

————. *Garden Shrubs and Their Histories.* London: Studio Vista Ltd., 1964.

————. *The Quest for Plants: A History of the Horticultural Explorers.* London: Studio Vista Ltd., 1969.

Corbitt, David Leroy, ed. *Explorations, Descriptions, and Attempted Settlements of Carolina 1584–1590.* Rev. ed. Raleigh, N. C.: State Department of Archives and History, 1953.

Correll, Donovan Stewart, and Johnston, Marshall Conring. *Manual of the Vascular Plants of Texas.* Renner, Tex.: Texas Research Foundation, 1970.

Cruickshank, Helen Gere, ed. *John and William Bartram's America: Selections from the Writings of the Early Philadelphia Naturalists.* New York: Devin–Adair Co., 1957.

Darlington, William. *Memorials of John Bartram and Humphrey Marshall, with Notices of their Botanical Contemporaries* (1849). Reprint ed. with an introduction by Joseph Ewan. New York: Hafner, 1967.

Darrow, George M. *The Strawberry: History, Breeding, and Physiology.* New York: Holt, Rinehart and Winston, 1966.

Davis, Burke. *A Williamsburg Galaxy.* Williamsburg, Va.: Colonial Williamsburg, 1968.

DeWolf, Gordon P., and Favretti, Rudy F. *Colonial Gardens.* Barre, Mass.: Barre Publishers, 1972.

Drewitt, F. Dawtrey. *The Romance of the Apothecaries' Garden at Chelsea.* Cambridge: University Press, 1928.

Duncan, Wilbur H., and Foote, Leonard E. *Wildflowers of the Southeastern United States.* Athens, Ga.: University of Georgia Press, 1975.

Dutton, Joan Parry. *Enjoying America's Gardens*. New York: Reynal & Co., 1958.

———. *The Flower World of Williamsburg*. Williamsburg, Va.: Colonial Williamsburg, 1962.

Eifert, Virginia S. *Tall Trees and Far Horizons: Adventures and Discoveries of Early Botanists in America*. New York: Dodd, Mead & Co., 1965.

Ewan, Joseph, and Ewan, Nesta. *John Banister and His Natural History of Virginia, 1678–1692*. Urbana, Ill.: University of Illinois Press, 1970.

Fernald, Merritt Lyndon. *Gray's Manual of Botany*. 8th ed. New York: American Book Co., 1950.

Fithian, Philip Vickers. *Journal & Letters of Philip Vickers Fithian, 1773–1774: A Plantation Tutor of the Old Dominion*. Edited by Hunter Dickinson Farish. Williamsburg, Va.: Colonial Williamsburg, 1957.

Foster, Gertrude B. *Herbs for Every Garden*. Rev. ed. New York: E. P. Dutton, 1973.

Fowells, F. A. *Silvics of Forest Trees of the United States*. Agriculture Handbook no. 271. Washington, D. C.: U. S. Department of Agriculture, 1965.

Gillis, William T. "The Septematics and Ecology of Poison-Ivy and the Poison-Oaks (Toxicodendron, Anacardiaceae)." *Rhodora*, LXXIII (1971), pp. 72–159, 161–237, 370–443, 465–540.

Grieve, Mrs. M. *A Modern Herbal*. 2 vols. London: Jonathan Cape, 1931.

Hadfield, Miles. *Gardening in Britain*. London: Hutchison & Co. Ltd., 1960.

———. *Pioneers in Gardening*. London: Routledge & Kegan Paul, 1955.

———. *Topiary and Ornamental Hedges: Their History and Cultivation*. London: Adam & Charles Black, 1971.

Hardin, James W., and Arena, Jay M. *Human Poisoning from Native and Cultivated Plants*. Durham, N. C.: Duke University Press, 1969.

Harrar, Ellwood S., and Harrar, J. George. *Guide to Southern Trees*. Reprint ed. New York: Dover, 1962.

Harvey, John H. *Early Gardening Catalogues*. London: Phillimore, 1972.

Harvill, A. M., Jr. *Spring Flora of Virginia*. Parsons, W. Va.:

McClain Printing Co., 1970.

Hatch, Charles E., Jr. "Mulberry Trees and Silkworms: Sericulture in Early Virginia." *Virginia Magazine of History and Biography,* LXV (January 1957), pp. 3–61.

Henrey, Blanche. *British Botanical and Horticultural Literature before 1800.* 3 vols. London: Oxford University Press, 1975.

Hillier and Sons. *Hilliers Manual of Trees and Shrubs.* Newton Abbot, Devon: David & Charles, 1972.

Jefferson, Thomas. *Thomas Jefferson's Garden Book, 1766–1824.* Edited by Edwin Morris Betts. Philadelphia: American Philosophical Society, 1944.

————. *Notes on the State of Virginia.* Edited by William Peden. Chapel Hill, N. C.: University of North Carolina Press, 1955.

Kidd, Mary Maytham. *Wild Flowers of the Cape Peninsula.* 2nd ed. Cape Town: Oxford University Press, 1973.

Kocher, A. Lawrence, and Dearstyne, Howard. *Colonial Williamsburg: Its Buildings and Gardens.* Williamsburg, Va.: Colonial Williamsburg, 1949.

Leighton, Ann. *Early American Gardens: "for Meate or Medicine."* Boston: Houghton Mifflin Co., 1970.

Long, Robert W., and Lakela, Olga. *A Flora of Tropical Florida: A Manual of the Seed Plants and Ferns of Southern Peninsular Florida.* Coral Gables, Fla.: University of Miami Press, 1971.

Peattie, Donald Culross, ed. *A Natural History of Trees of Eastern and Central North America.* Boston: Houghton Mifflin Co., 1966.

Perry, Frances. *Flowers of the World.* London: Hamlyn, 1972.

Polunin, Oleg. *Flowers of Europe.* London: Oxford University Press, 1969.

————. and Smythies, B. E. *Flowers of South-West Europe.* London: Oxford University Press, 1973.

Rickett, Harold William. *Wild Flowers of the United States.* Vol. I, pts. 1–2: *The Northeastern States.* New York: McGraw-Hill, 1966.

Smith, A. W., and Stearn, W. T. *A Gardener's Dictionary of Plant Names: A Handbook on the Origin & Meaning of Some Plant Names.* New York: St. Martin's Press, 1972.

Stafleu, F. A., et al., eds. *International Code of Botanical Nomenclature, Adopted by the Eleventh International Botanical Congress,*

Seattle, August 1969. Regnum Vegetabile, LXXXII. Utrecht, 1972.

Stupka, Arthur. *Wildflowers in Color.* New York: Harper & Row, 1965.

Swem, E. G., ed. "Brothers of the Spade: Correspondence of Peter Collinson, of London, and of John Custis, of Williamsburg, Virginia, 1734-1746." American Antiquarian Society, *Proceedings,* LVIII (1958), pp. 17-190.

Synge, Patrick M., ed. *Royal Horticultural Society Supplement to the Dictionary of Gardening.* Rev. ed. London: Clarendon Press, 1969.

Taylor, Norman, ed. *Taylor's Encyclopedia of Gardening.* 4th ed. Boston: Houghton Mifflin Co., 1961.

Taylor, Raymond L. *Plants of Colonial Days.* Williamsburg, Va.: Colonial Williamsburg, 1952.

Webber, Ronald. *The Early Horticulturists.* New York: Augustus M. Kelley, 1968.

Wyman, Donald. *Shrubs and Vines for American Gardens.* Rev. ed. New York: The Macmillan Co., 1969.

Index

MENTION IN letter Fm of 17 FEB 1900 Cynthia Collis sent SEEDS for Willie's Grave

[191]